CHRISTn
MERRY CHRISTMAS
And
Thank you
Bob Rein
N96T5R

S0-AKX-734

# Bonanza Around the World

## By
## Dennis Stewart

# Bonanza Around the World

## By
## Dennis Stewart

First Edition
First Printing
© Copyright 1998, Dennis Stewart

Printed in the United States of America. All rights reserved. No part of this book may be reproduced or transmitted in any form or by any means, electronic or mechanical, including photocopying, recording or by any information storage or retrieval system, except by a reviewer who may quote brief passages in a review to be printed in a magazine, newspaper or newsletter, without permission in writing from the publisher. The publisher takes no responsibility for use of materials in, nor for the factual accuracy of any portion of, this book.

ISBN: 1-891118-28-5

Published by
**Wind Canyon Publishing, Inc.**
P.O. Box 1445
Niceville, FL 32588-1445

Editor: George Jaquith
Layout/Design: Becky Jaquith
Cover Design: **Wind Canyon Publishing, Inc.** ©1998
Photos provided by Dennis Stewart and Bob Reiss

**Wind Canyon Publishing, Inc.** offers other book titles. **Wind Canyon, Inc.** offers software applications work related to book publishing, including converting titles to multimedia CD-ROM discs and other computer formats. For further information, including details regarding the submission of manuscripts, contact the above address.

For Lois —

The Love of My Life

# INTRODUCTION

The rain squall hits the Bonanza's windshield like a fire hose. The aircraft rocks and shudders in turbulence as we look down at twenty-five foot waves below. We are at nine hundred feet over the Gulf of Alaska in a single-engine light aircraft and at least one hundred and fifty miles from shore. A giant low pressure storm covers the entire region and we are in the middle of it. Strong headwinds up to seventy-five knots push our ground speed to a virtual crawl — we are down to about ninety-six knots.

There's a light! Through the rain and wisps of the cloud base we see a small dot of amber glowing on the surface less than a mile away, dead ahead. A fishing boat emerges as it crests one of the enormous breakers and goes almost vertical as it slides down the other side of the wave. How do those sailors manage to take that kind of beating hour after hour? We fly over them and continue on.

We are down at this low altitude in an only partly successful attempt to maintain visual flight conditions. This morning in Anchorage the weather forecast for our intended route to Ketchikan predicted moderate to severe icing from 1,500 to 14,000 feet. The Bonanza has no anti-icing equipment beyond an electric propeller heater and there is no way we could file a normal flight plan in these conditions. The weather people also predicted that the giant storm would stick around for at least three days. Bob Reiss, the owner and pilot in command of Bonanza 9675R, has decided to go VFR rather then wait out the storm. We are below controlled airspace and don't require an Air Traffic Control clearance.

Now, three hours into the flight, in and out of heavy rain and brushing against a base of dark clouds while bucking gale force winds, I have my doubts about the wisdom of this venture. As copilot and navigator, Bob expects me to keep track of our whereabouts and lay a course that will bring us to a safe arrival before we run out of fuel. With the winds blowing as they are, it is not certain we can make Ketchikan with a safe margin in the tanks. We'll worry about that when we near land and start checking the weather at various airports. Right now, I'm thinking about what would happen if an engine failure forced us to ditch into these roiling seas.

From our low altitude there would be no time to get into the rubber immersion suits stowed behind our seats, so even if we lived through the water landing (an unlikely prospect) our survival in those icy waves would be limited to only a matter of minutes. I keep these thoughts to myself as we fly on.

I consult the Global Positioning System (GPS) receiver in my left hand. We are on course, past Middleton Island, and headed almost due east for a point about twenty miles offshore from Ocean Cape where Alaska's panhandle begins. From there we will turn southeast and parallel the rugged coastline as we search for better weather. Thank God for GPS or we would really be in trouble.

What am I, Dennis Stewart, a sixty-year old, out of shape, retired federal employee, doing here? I am certainly not having a lot of fun at the moment. I have enough experience in the air and have read enough aviation accident reports to fully comprehend the various scenarios, many of them calamitous, that can result from getting yourself into a situation like this. It has been an intricate chain of events that led us to this place, at this time, flying in an around-the-world air race.

Starting in San Diego twenty-eight days ago, we have flown to Canada and across the Atlantic. The Bonanza has passed over North Africa, the Middle East, and through the dust of India. We have seen the jungles of Southeast Asia and a sunset over the Philippine Sea. All of Japan, the Kamchatka Peninsula, and the Bering Sea are behind us and now, if our fortunes hold, two more legs of our journey will see us back home.

\* \* \* \* \* \* \* \* \* \*

I had no idea at the time that I would write a book about this adventure, but friends and family encouraged me that this is a story worth telling, with memories and relationships worth preserving in print. Fortunately my publisher agreed. So with the benefit of my diary, notes and conversations with Bob Reiss, this book developed. Oh, and despite what you will read about my Kodak "Smilesaver" as we cleared Customs in Agra, India, for the most part it performed nicely.

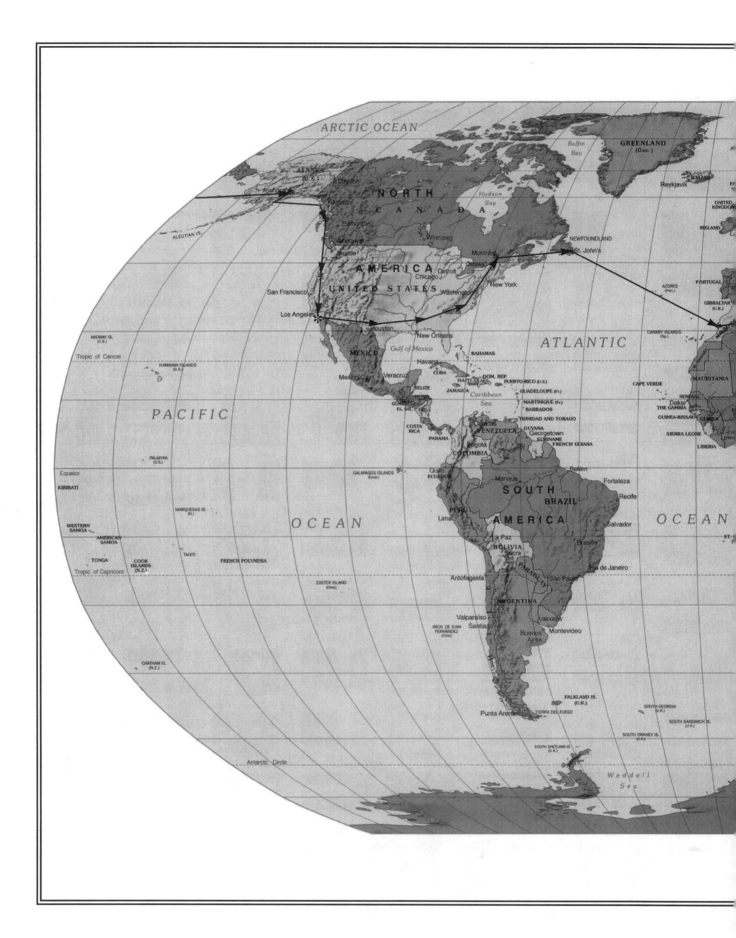

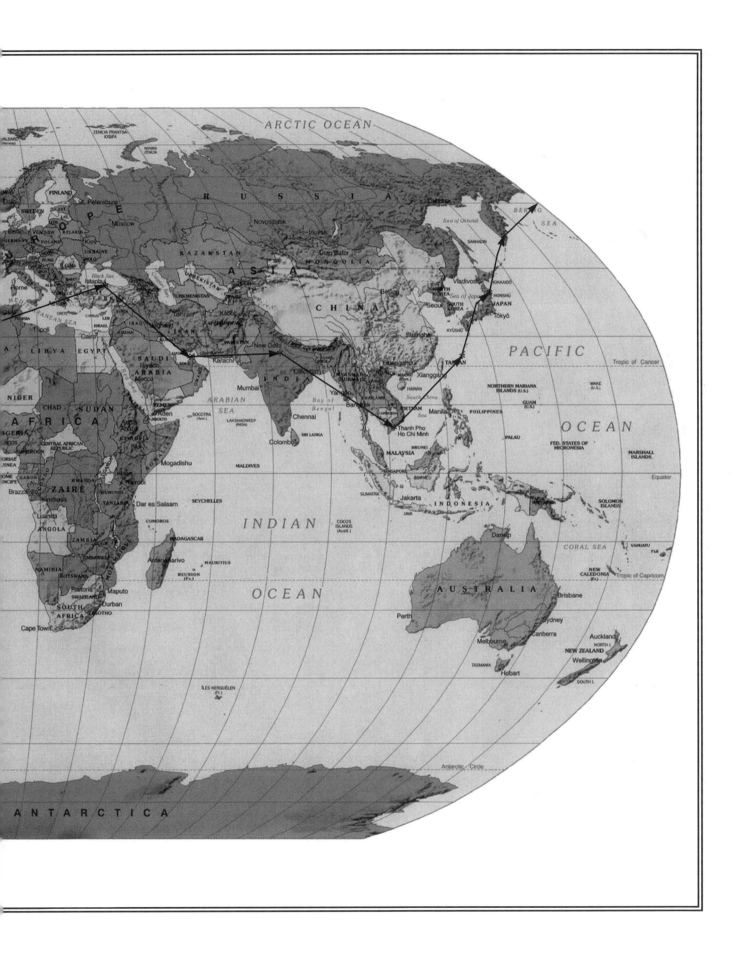

# CONTENTS

# CHAPTER 1

# PREPARATIONS

NOVEMBER 1993. My wife, Lois, and I live quietly in a suburb of San Diego in the sixth year of my retirement as a civilian employee of the Department of the Navy. Our two daughters are grown and on their own. I read a lot, play with the World War II aircraft of the Confederate Air Force, bang on the piano, and am happily inefficient in the use of my time. A native Californian, I don't miss the change of seasons or the colors of eastern foliage. I am content with the climate of my native region.

I collect the day's mail and among the bills and advertisements is a letter from a French organization called "Arc en Ciel" (Rainbow). It contains a crew entry form for the "Round the World Air Race '94" beginning in Montreal on 1 May next year. I can guess what this is about. My good friend Bob Reiss is behind it. I call Bob and he confirms that he has entered his A36 Beechcraft prop-jet Bonanza in the race and that the entry form is his invitation to me to be his copilot/navigator.

None of this really surprises me. Bob has been bitten by the long-range flying bug and has contracted a disease that is both incurable and expensive. Last year he and I flew his Bonanza as part of the Round the World Air Rally. We departed Santa Monica on July 4th and returned home twenty-two days later. With twelve other aircraft we crossed the United States, flew to Goose Bay, Labrador, and over the Atlantic via Greenland and Iceland, proceeded to Southend near London and, after stopping in Helsinki, entered Russia and flew its entire length to Anadyr in eastern Siberia. From there, we went to Anchorage, Ketchikan (Alaska), Eugene (Oregon), then home. It was a magnificent, once in a lifetime, adventure with no serious incidents. The airplane performed flawlessly and he and I became a true aviation team with Bob handling the controls, engineering, and radios, and me doing the flight planning and navigating. Despite the crude accommodations and food in parts of Russia, we had a great time. The endless forests and mountains of the great Taiga of

1

Siberia were a sight to hold in memory forever.

Now Bob wanted to do it again, only this time the long way. Our first circumnavigation had been mainly at high latitudes, above 45 degrees north, a mere 17,000+ miles. This time the route would take us far closer to the equator and would require flying over 21,000 nautical miles in thirty days.

We have a long talk. I have some misgivings — after all, we had done it once perfectly and had nothing more to prove. Was it wise to press our luck by doing it again? Bob is a good salesman and his enthusiasm wins me over. I agree to go. My misgivings were very thin anyway.

One of the few things I know about the route at this point is that we will cross the Atlantic from St. John's, Newfoundland to the Azores. I go to my atlas. Jesus! That leg is near to thirteen hundred nautical miles over open ocean. We are going to need more fuel capacity this time.

\* \* \* \* \* \* \* \* \* \* \* \* \* \* \*

Before going further with this account it is best to let you know something about the three main players involved:

**ROBERT REISS** (sounds like "Reese"). Bob is a resident of San Diego. Raised in the tenements of New York City, he holds a Bachelors Degree in Industrial Engineering from the GMI Engineering and Management Institute and the first Bioengineering Degree given by Columbia University. He is the Founder, Chairman, CEO, and a principal patent holder of InterVentional Technologies, which manufactures medical devices that will mechanically clean out your blood vessels from the inside. He and his wife, Claire, have two beautiful daughters. He is fluent in Mandarin Chinese, which he learned at the Army Language School when he was preparing for his military stint as an intelligence agent. He is also fluent in Latin and is well read in the classics. This walking admixture of inventor, business executive and scholar has many other attributes. He has an engaging manner and a sharp sense of humor, yet has little time for fools. Stupidity and laziness make him angry. Quietly generous with his wealth, he funds

*The Author (L) and Bob Reiss, owner of the A36 Bonanza prop-jet.*

the Reisung Foundation which supports a wide variety of local charities, medical institutions and museums. He is an accomplished public speaker and is frequently called on to address business groups on finance and other matters. Widely read in world history, he loves to spend hours in discussions of the past. Although he does not use alcohol in any form, he is a world class coffee drinker. He is the most interesting and complex man I have ever known.

Bob has been flying for thirty years and has over 5,000 hours in the air with commercial and instrument ratings. He is also certified as an instrument instructor. He loves airplanes and everything about them and uses his Bonanza frequently for business and pleasure in flights all over the United States and Canada. He owns and flies two other aircraft: a Cessna 195 and a beautifully restored N2S-1 Stearman biplane. As a life member of the Confederate Air Force, he purchased and donated a fully restored FM-2 "Wildcat" WWII Navy fighter to the organization and remains the principal sponsor of that aircraft's maintenance and operation. He was 55 years old when we went on this flight in 1994. Bob and I met in 1984 through our mutual enthusiasm for warbirds. We hit it off at once and have been friends ever since.

**DENNIS STEWART.** Born and reared in Bell, California, a suburb of Los Angeles. Blue collar parents. After two years at Compton Junior College I enlisted in the U.S. Air Force in 1953 as an Aviation Cadet. Trained in T-6 "Texans" and B-25 "Mitchells" in flight school, I was assigned to the Military Air Transport Service as a pilot on C-124 "Globemaster" four-engine transports. I flew many missions in C-124s across the Pacific Ocean carrying cargo to and from the Far East. After my time in the service I completed college with a BA in History from San Francisco State College. In 1960 I took a job with the Federal Aviation Agency as an Air Traffic Controller at the Los Angeles Air Route Traffic Control Center, transferring to Anchorage Center/Radar Approach Control in 1962. Fearing for my sanity if I stayed in ATC, I wrangled a job in the training department of the FAA's regional office in Anchorage in 1964 and began a career in personnel management. Switching from the FAA to the Department of the Navy in 1967, I worked in Japan, Philadelphia, and finally San Diego, where I wound up my federal career in 1988 holding the ponderous title of Director, Southwest Region, Office of Civilian Personnel Management, Department of the Navy. I never lost my love of aviation, and hold a commercial multi-engine and instrument rating and have slightly over 2,000 hours in my logbook. I was 60 years old when we made the flight in 1994.

**A36 BEECHCRAFT BONANZA N9675R.** This aircraft, manufactured in 1989, became Bob Reiss's ultimate flying dream. During his long flying career Bob has one way or another survived ten (yes, 10) catastrophic engine failures. Grimly determined to break this pattern he studied all his options and decided to obtain the most reliable single-engined aircraft in the world. [In case you are wondering why he didn't get a twin-engine aircraft, the answer is he doesn't like them.] He settled upon an A36 Bonanza with the Soloy conversion to a turboprop engine.

He bought a factory-fresh A36 and had it flown to the Seattle area where the conversions were being done at the time. The converted aircraft, one of

*The instrument panel and controls of N9675R.*

*Bob Reiss standing next to his A36 Bonanza prop-jet.*

fewer than forty in the world, with its nose section elongated to accommodate the B-17 Allison jet engine, is a formidable flying machine. It has the equivalent of 420 horsepower up front, climbs like an interceptor, and cruises close to 200 knots (230 mph) at 13,000 feet. Inside, the noise level is low and vibration is almost nonexistent. Most importantly for Bob, the engine is twenty-five times more reliable than a piston engine. The cabin is not pressurized. For avionics it has a sophisticated autopilot system, three VORs plus DME, two radios, ADF, Stormscope, transponder, ILS coupled to the autopilot, and a fuel management computer. It is a flying magic carpet capable of going anywhere.

* * * * * * * * * * * * * *

Two weeks after the entry form arrived, I get my hands on the first two bulletins issued by the race organizers in Paris. Now I know the general routing. Starting in Montreal on May 1st, the race will proceed via Newfoundland, the Azores, Morocco, Istanbul, Dubai in the United Arab Emirates, Agra (India), Saigon, Taiwan, Sendai (Japan),

Petropavlovsk (Russia), Anchorage, Calgary, and return to Montreal. In over half these locations we will get one or two days rest. Now I can start the flight planning. Bob and I have conferred and, as before, agreed that I will do all the route planning and assemble the necessary charts and equipment while Bob will see to the conversion of his Bonanza to a long-range world cruiser.

My first step is to visit David Weiss at Aviation Publications Service in Del Mar, just up the coast. Operating from his house, David sells aviation charts and publications of every description. For about $50.00 I buy Defense Mapping Agency (DMA) instrument charts for the entire route. These charts are outdated but will do for planning purposes until we get a complete set of current Jeppesen charts just before the race begins. For another $85.00 I also purchase a set of DMA Operational Navigation Charts (ONC) that cover our entire route. These are four-color terrain charts, beautifully printed on heavy paper, that show all elevations and relevant features of the earth's surface, both natural and man-made. Their scale is 1,000,000 to 1. These ONC charts are too big to unfold in a cramped cockpit so

I will crop them down to 100NM either side of our intended course and accordion fold them for my use. They also show all known airports, and before we start I will mark them with the latitude and longitude of each airfield so I will be able to quickly punch the coordinates into the Global Positioning System in the event of an emergency anytime during the trip over land.

For the long over-water portions of our flight (the Atlantic crossing, the leg from Saigon to Taiwan, and the Bering Sea) I make up complete dead reckoning flight plans that include all latitude/longitude checkpoint coordinates, the true course for each segment taken off oceanic charts with a plotter, the compass variation and true heading for each segment, and the distance in nautical miles. There are vacant blocks in the plans for wind direction and velocity to be filled in at the weather briefings. All this is done so that if the GPS should fail for any reason on one of these legs and we are out of range of ground navigation aids, I can fall back on dead reckoning navigation to get us close enough to our destination to pick up a VOR or ADF radio beacon. I will have my old-fashioned E6B manual flight calculator with me that can provide wind drift solutions. Bob says he feels better with someone in the cockpit who has experience in ocean flying, but my experience is almost forty years old. I go to my old military footlocker and dig out the 1950s USAF manual *Air Navigation For Pilots* and study such arcane subjects as double drift calculations, how to determine the point of no return, and radius of action problems. Also of great help is Louise Sacchi's *Ocean Flying*, a book now out of print.

I borrow Bob's Garmin 100 GPS receiver. Sitting at my desk at home I can plug it in the wall with a special transformer, set it for "Simulation," and begin checking out each route. The Garmin 100 is programmed with the entire Jeppesen world data base. Every known radio navigation aid, and every non-secret military or civilian airport on the planet is somehow contained in its innards. The entire unit is only 7x5x4 inches and weighs about a pound. It knows the magnetic variation of every spot on earth. It can calculate distance, ground speed, true air speed, estimated time, magnetic bearings, altitude, and the winds aloft. Once it acquires three or more of the military satellites orbiting above, it knows exactly where it is on earth within thirty yards and can tell you on its screen how to get to anywhere you want to go. It is an electronic miracle — the instrument navigators have been dreaming of since they took to the seas and oceans.

Using the instrument charts I fill out a separate sheet for each day's projected flight using my best guess for the exact route we will fly. I put the ICAO (International Civil Aviation Organization) four-letter identifier for the departure, destination, and alternate airports, each airway, the radio fixes along the airway, the distance between each fix, and the minimum IFR altitude for each segment of the route. These will be of use not only for navigation but also in preparing the ICAO flight plans required for clearance. It is far better, and often required, to file an instrument flight plan regardless of the weather when flying international routes. That way, at least in theory, everyone knows who you are, where you are going, and how you intend to get there. It's a good idea not to surprise air traffic controllers, military defense radar operators, or customs officials.

Another visit to Aviation Publications in Del Mar has equipped me with three important reference works for international flying:

1. The ICAO booklet *Location Indicators* which lists the four-letter identifier for every airport and FIR (Flight Information Region) in the world. They are listed alphabetically by name and also by their four-letter designations.

2. The Department of Defense booklet *General Planning* which lays out the rules of international flying, how to file ICAO flight plans, and how to read international weather reports and forecasts, which are different from the FAA format. It also describes international emergency procedures.

3. The D.O.D. *Notices to Airmen* (NOTAMS), published every three months, which advises of local procedures and restrictions for each Flight Information Region and airport in the world.

Going over the NOTAMS I find intriguing pieces of information such as:

1. In many Arab countries it is illegal to enter their airspace if the flight originated in Israel, or if your aircraft was built there.

2. Published magnetic variation values for the Azores may be "significantly different" due to vol-

canic activity.

3. When flying in Greece you must maintain at least 5,000 feet over the Acropolis to avoid causing vibration damage.

4. Ankara (Turkey) and Nicosia (Cyprus) Air Control Centers are not in contact with each other although they share a common boundary. All flights must contact them at least ten minutes before entering their FIRs.

5. All aircraft in the Cairo FIR are required to report bird concentrations or migrations.

6. If you are staying overnight in Hong Kong during the period May to November, the authorities must have your hotel and room number so you can evacuate your aircraft in the event of a typhoon.

I summarize these publications in a number of long memos to Bob so he can appreciate the complications we may encounter on our journey.

The question of visas arises. On our previous trip we needed none for Canada, Greenland, Iceland, or any European country, only for Russia. [Half the distance we traveled was in Russia and Siberia which at latitude 45 degrees north covers 179 degrees of longitude. If you don't believe this, look at a polar projection of the earth.] This time we will be landing in about eleven different countries, not all of them good buddies with the USA. Who requires a visa and who doesn't?

I get the phone number of International Visa Services in Los Angeles and talk to a Mr. Rogers. When I describe our trip he rejects my business out of hand as too complicated. He is very helpful, however, in informing me of who requires what. It seems we will need visas for the United Arab Emirates, India, Vietnam, and Russia. He even gives me the telephone number for the Vietnamese Mission to the United Nations (the Vietnamese have no embassy in the United States). I call them and they are most cooperative.

They send us applications and we fill them out and send in passport photos, copies of our passports, and two checks for $90.00. In two weeks we have our Vietnam visas. A call to the Indian Consulate in San Francisco gets similar results at $70.00 each. About this time we hear from Arc en Ciel, the race organizers, that they will handle the visas for the Emirates and Russia for all of us. The visa problem is solved.

In one of the bulletins from Arc en Ciel, the Director, Bernard Lamy, informs us that negotiations to land the racers in Taiwan have broken down for "political reasons." Now the race will be routed from Vietnam to Okinawa, then on to Sendai, Japan. This news sends me back to the charts for more replotting.

While all this is going on, Bob has been very busy with the Bonanza. He has made a list of spare parts, including one each nose and main tires and tube that will be taken along. Thanks to the elongated nose of the turboprop conversion, there is ample storage space in the nose compartments for these items including four quarts of the special engine oil needed for the Allison. The next concern is fuel capacity. The jet engine burns far more fuel than the Bonanza's original power plant. It will consume 160 pounds (23.8 gallons) per hour. He already has a 90

*N9675R auxiliary cabin tank installation (90-gallon capacity) with the emergency air pressure pump on top.*

*Good views of the tip-tanks.*

*Below:*

*Fueling a tip-tank — a need for range accommodated by safe engineering.*

*Frank Haile's design tip-tank compared to standard tip-tank.*

gallon (three plus hours) auxiliary tank we used for the world trip last time and it will be installed in the rear cabin after the seats are taken out. It has its own electric pump to feed fuel into the main tanks and we will carry along a large volume low-pressure hand pump (the kind you use to blow up large beach toys) to pressurize the tank if the electrical pump fails. But this auxiliary tank will not be enough. We are going to need a straight line no wind range of about 2,000 nautical miles (2,330 statute miles) to ensure a safe margin. The Bonanza's main tanks in the wings hold 74 gallons. We will need another 100 gallons aboard and the only way that much fuel can be carried is in the wingtips. Any more in the cabin would disrupt our center of gravity too much.

Bob contacts Frank Haile in Texas. Frank has a cache of surplus Air Force belly tanks that have been shortened and can be adapted to make large capacity tip-tanks for light aircraft. Frank is not giving them away but wants a hefty price. After negotiations Frank agrees to ship two tanks to Bob right away but

there are many unexplained delays. These delays will eventually jam Bob up with the Federal Aviation Administration.

*N9675R — checking things out prior to departure.*

the mathematical and structural analysis required, that the FAA approves the change. The only structural modification will be the addition of inboard to outboard stringers between the two outboard ribs. The tip-tank load is therefore spread over a larger area. Each new wingtip tank has a capacity of 100 gallons. The aviation world calls them *Dolly Partons* (although I can't imagine why). The FAA approves them for no more than 50 gallons each. All this has taken much time and the final approval on the tanks comes just a few days before we are to leave San Diego. There will be no chance to test the new tanks at full load and in flight until we actually depart. Bob does test them at 20 gallons each and tests the dual fuel transfer pumps. He discovers and

Any major structural change to a certificated aircraft must be approved by the FAA. These new tanks, when attached to the wingtips, will change the dynamics of the pressures acting on the wing. The FAA seems as much concerned with the stresses on the ground as in the air. Are the wings strong enough to support the extra weight without sustaining damage while maneuvering on the ground over rough terrain as well as in heavy turbulence? It is not until Bob, at his own expense, calls in a DER (Designated Engineering Representative) with extensive Beech aircraft experience and has him do all

*Another view of N9675R, mostly loaded and prior to departure.*

fixes a glitch in the tip-tank fuel quantity gauges. We plan to accomplish the full load test by gradually working from 20 gallons each to 50 gallons each (and beyond) as we proceed.

During the last month before departure Bob and I agree on certain extra emergency equipment to bring along beyond the ocean survival equipment required by the Canadian Ministry of Transport for flying the Atlantic. We are going to be way over the Bonanza's design maximum gross weight and we must keep it basic and simple. We decide on mosquito nets, water purification tablets, some pain pills, sun blocker, insect repellent, a can opener, flashlights, cold medicine, chapstick, a sewing kit, two gallons of water and a first aid kit.

Both of us have consulted doctors about immunizations. Although none is required for any country we will visit, we both know that if either of us becomes incapacitated it could ruin the trip. At Kaiser-Permanente, my HMO, the Travel Advisory Service listens to my proposed itinerary with some amazement. They are more concerned about malaria than anything else because it is now endemic in most parts of India. After studying the matter they come up with the following recommendations:

Immunizations:
    Tetanus
    Diphtheria
    Immune Globulin
    Meningococcal vaccine
Prescriptions:
    Doxycycline (to prevent malaria)
    Vivotif oral Typhoid vaccine
    Septra DS (for severe diarrhea)

I agree to their advice and take them all. Bob's doctor recommends much the same thing. In addition, Bob is a great believer in taking a daily dose of two tetracycline pills while traveling in areas with questionable water or food. Upon departure Bob has managed to obtain 1,000 250mg capsules.

On March 26th I go to Montreal alone to represent our team at the planning meeting called by the race organizers. At the Montreal airport I run into Gordon and Dawn Barstch, old friends from the Around the World Rally of 1992. They are a Canadian couple, living in Hawaii, who fly a beautiful Cessna 421 twin, *Kona Wind*. They too have

caught the long-range bug. We share a taxi into town.

The meeting is chaired by Bernard Lamy of Paris, race organizer and head of Arc en Ciel. He is a big handsome fellow, about 60 years old, whose English is accented but very fluent. He seems to have his full share of French male ego and has little patience with any disagreements. He outlines the rules of the race.

A. It will be sanctioned by the ICAO as part of their 50th anniversary observance. It has been approved as a Category I FAI event. Speed records between cities may be claimed.

B. There will be three categories of racers, each competing only within their group:
    (1) Normally aspirated piston aircraft.
    (2) Turbocharged piston aircraft.
    (3) Jet turboprop powered aircraft.

C. All racers will be judged by how close to, or above, they can make each leg compared to the reference speed from their aircraft's Pilot Operating Handbook. The accumulated times from each leg will be totaled to determine the overall winners. The reference speed will be:
    (1) 75% power speed of the aircraft at fastest altitude and at max normal gross weight for piston powered aircraft.
    (2) Max high speed cruise for turboprops.

This formula ruins any chances Bob has for competing well in the race. Although there is no published max high cruise speed for the turboprop converted Bonanza, Lamy will make an arbitrary decision, reasonably enough, that it is 200 knots. At the weights at which we will be taking off, and the increased induced drag of the huge tip-tanks, Bob will not be able to come close to 200. He already knows this but we will go along anyway just for the pleasure of being part of the whole venture.

I sense that most of the entrants, unlike us, are dead serious competitors and are already attempting to psyche out each other. They are mostly Americans, but other teams are from Belgium, Switzerland, Norway, Canada, France, and India. All have U.S. built aircraft.

For the rest of the day Bernard goes over the details of the arrangements at each stopover of the race. The final schedule you'll see on the next page.

The distance between stopover cities is so great

# FINAL SCHEDULE

| May  1 Sunday | Montreal to St. John's | 947NM |
|---|---|---|
| May  2 Monday | St. John's to Marrakech, Morocco | 2483NM |
| | (Stop for fuel in Azores) | |
| May  3 Tuesday | Land in Marrakech | |
| May  4 Wednesday | Day off | |
| May  5 Thursday | Marrakech to Istanbul, Turkey | 1820NM |
| May  6 Friday | Day off | |
| May  7 Saturday | Istanbul to Dubai, UAE | 1620NM |
| May  8 Sunday | Day off | |
| May  9 Monday | Dubai to Agra, India | 1230NM |
| May 10 Tuesday | Day off | |
| May 11 Wednesday | Agra to Ho Chi Minh City, Vietnam | 1860NM |
| May 12 Thursday | Day off | |
| May 13 Friday | Day off | |
| May 14 Saturday | Ho Chi Minh City to Naha, Okinawa | 1564NM |
| May 15 Sunday | Day off | |
| May 16 Monday | Day off | |
| May 17 Tuesday | Naha to Sendai, Japan | 1202NM |
| May 18 Wednesday | Day off | |
| May 19 Thursday | Sendai to Petropavlovsk, Russia | 1213NM |
| May 20 Friday | Day off | |
| May 21 Saturday | Petropavlovsk to Anchorage, Alaska | 1721NM |
| | (International Date Line) | |
| May 20 Friday | Land Anchorage | |
| May 21 Saturday | Day off | |
| May 22 Sunday | Anchorage to Calgary, Canada | 1319NM |
| May 23 Monday | Day off | |
| May 24 Tuesday | Calgary to Montreal | 1610NM |

in some cases that most of the racers will have to make interim fuel stops. They can choose when and where to do this but in almost all cases their race clock for that leg will keep running while they fuel. I don't like the sound of this. It will mean urgent calls to control towers to have fuel trucks waiting and the kind of frantic runaround on the ground that can lead to mistakes and accidents. Thank goodness Bob and I will not be serious racers. When we stop for fuel we can have a bite, stretch our legs, and get a weather briefing before departing again.

The availability and price of aviation gasoline is a problem. Jet aircraft now own the world. The piston racers must specify how much gas they will need at each refueling spot and be prepared to pay from $2.70 to $8.00 per gallon. Russian avgas (Vietnam and Petropavlovsk) is not suitable for American engines and special arrangements must be made to fuel up elsewhere, or in the case of Petropavlovsk, have the gasoline barged over from Alaska. We kerosene burners are more fortunate. Jet fuel is plentiful all over and will be in the range of $1.20 to $1.50 a gallon. All gasoline and fuel must be paid for in U.S. cash at the time of purchase, and no change will be given by the dealers. There is one exception to this. One of the race's corporate sponsors is Indian Oil. They will contribute 40,000 rupees and Bernard Lamy is stuck with it — he can't take them out of the country. We are to let him pay for fuel in Agra with rupees, and reimburse him for our purchase.

I have to hand it to Bernard Lamy. He *is* Arc en Ciel, and it is obvious that his passion for aviation is a lifelong pursuit. Organizing a race like this, arranging for all the fuel stops, hotels, meals, governmental authorizations (bribes?), and the thousand other details that must go with the effort is a monumental undertaking. He is assisted by his wife, Maryse, and several sons, nephews, and in-laws (I never get them all straight). In turn, the entrants must cough up $10,000 per aircraft and $10,000 per person. This will pay for race organization and all hotels, meals, landing fees, ground tours, and beer and wine. Entrants must buy their own fuel and hard liquor.

Bernard wants all aircraft to have names. It is decided that Bob and I will be flying in the "Spirit of San Diego," a title I never hear used again.

All aircraft are to assemble on April 29th at St.

Hubert Airport, Montreal. The race will begin on the morning of May 1st.

## FLASHBACK I

*[Note: Throughout this work the Author has inserted a number of "Flashback" episodes describing incidents with which he was connected during his time in the US Air Force. They are offered so that younger readers will have some sense of what it was like flying in aviation's Golden Age. Aviation's Golden Age was, of course, the 1950s.]*

## "HOTSHOTS"

HONDO AIR BASE, TEXAS, JULY 1954. Our hero was an Aviation Cadet at Primary Flight School. On this particularly hot and muggy day he was aloft in the front seat of a T-6G "Texan" trainer taking an acrobatic lesson. His civilian instructor, Virgil Geyser, was in the rear seat. Our hero, along with three other fellow students, was known as one of "Geyser's Squirts."

"Okay," said Virgil. "That eight-point slow roll was.... well.... acceptable. Now climb to 7,000 and give me an Immelman."

An Immelman turn is a maneuver in which the aircraft does a half loop and rolls out to level flight at the top. It sounds easier than it is. At the top the plane's speed is very slow and the roll from inverted must be made quickly and smoothly to avoid a stall.

At 7,000 feet our hero began the two clearing turns, 180 degrees to the left and then 180 degrees to the right, specified in the training syllabus to make sure the area was clear of other aircraft. This done, he opened the throttle and went into a dive to reach the 200 mph required to begin the Immelman.

As he started the half loop the "G" forces caused the usual "grayout" to his vision. When the aircraft reached vertical and began to go over, his vision cleared. At that instant the blue sky in front was suddenly replaced by an expanse of aluminum! Another aircraft!

Instinctively he jammed the control stick forward and closed the throttle, missing the tail of a passing C-119 "Boxcar" by about twenty feet. The T-6, now dead vertical and with no power, stopped in mid-air, then began a tail slide backwards. The propeller came to a stop, then began winding up in reverse. Our hero put in full right rudder which caused the Texan to turn to the *left*. As the nose dropped and the aircraft entered a spin, the propeller stopped again, then started turning the normal way. As he recovered from the spin and opened the throttle once more the large amount of gasoline vapor that had accumulated in the engine during these gyrations now exploded out the exhaust ports with two tremendous tongues of flame which covered the canopy and scorched paint halfway to the tail.

Once the Texan was flying straight and level again, both the student and the instructor were quiet as they each reflected on their failure to see that other aircraft during the clearing turns. Finally Virgil said, "At least you've learned now why we ask you to keep the canopy closed during all acrobatic maneuvers."

The incident was never mentioned again by either of them.

# CHAPTER 2

# THE JOURNEY BEGINS

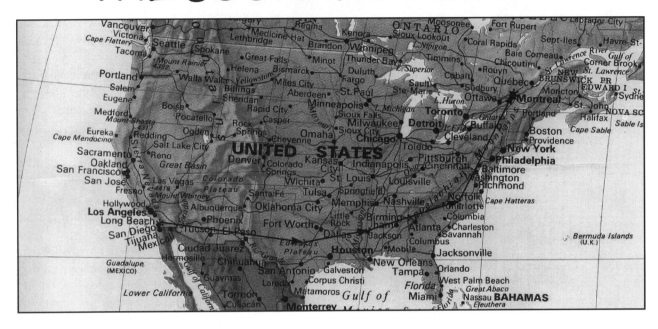

As the time for departure from San Diego nears there are hundreds of small but vital details to see to. Get a bar of antibacterial soap, a plastic soap dish and wash cloth. Get two rolls of toilet paper. Should I bring an umbrella? Is there an extra refill for the ballpoint? Be sure the wives have a complete itinerary of our hotels and the dates we will be in them. Get some fresh batteries for the flashlight. See your dentist. It goes on and on. We have agreed to hold our personal luggage to twenty-five pounds each because of overall weight considerations. We will be visiting Vietnam during its hot season, yet six days later we will be on the Kamchatka Peninsula where it will still be winter. I must be sure to include some thermal underwear. I make long lists and begin checking off items one by one.

I must get to the bank and draw out cash. Bob has made the same generous offer to me as he did for our 1992 trip. He will pay the entrance fee for both of us and buy all the fuel as we go along (If I had to pay my fair share, I couldn't go). He will be carry-

ing about $10,000 in cash on his person. I will pack $5,000 — half in cash, half in traveler's checks. You never know what you are going to run into, or what kind of a situation out of which you are going to have to buy your way. Both of us will carry our cash, passports and visas in moneybelts that fit under our shirts and rest at the small of our backs. These belts will never be more than a few feet away from us during the entire trip.

Bob has arranged to rent a life raft and other ocean survival gear required for flying the Atlantic. Single-engine aircraft are also required to have immersion suits for each person aboard. No one rents immersion suits in my size (I am 6'4" tall), so I must buy a special one. It costs $300 and arrives by Federal Express in time.

It is Monday, April 25th. We must leave tomorrow or the next day to have enough time to get to Montreal by the 29th. All preparations have been made except the final calculation of the Bonanza's weight and balance. The weather gods are not coop-

*April 26, 1994, the day of departure.  It is a cold day in San Diego.*

weigh each piece on a bathroom scale before it is stowed aboard. Using the balance moments from the aircraft handbook, Bob plots the center of gravity. We are so far over gross weight that he uses a blank piece of paper to project the lines off the chart in the handbook. The center of gravity looks okay.

Several friends, along with some of the mechanics who have been preparing the plane, are there to see us off. We thank them for their good wishes but ask them to leave us alone for these last few minutes of preparation. We don't want our concentration broken at some critical point and then forget something.

We are ready. The main tanks are full and the cabin auxiliary tank has 30 gallons. The tip-tanks

erating. The entire central region of the United States is a cauldron of tornadoes and thunderstorms. We don't want to test the tip-tanks in bad weather. The forecast for the next few days offers no improvement.

Early on Tuesday the 26th Bob calls and says we should depart today before it gets worse. We will try to skirt the worst of the weather by going south along the Gulf states then up the east coast. I get my gear together, say good-bye, and get over to Montgomery Field where the Bonanza is hangared. It is raining, which it is not supposed to do in San Diego this time of year. The wind is blowing hard and it's relatively cold. Bob is wearing a parka and knit cap. We spread out all our stuff on the hangar floor and

*Bob Reiss is smelling a fuel sample, an important pre-flight procedure.*

carry 20 gallons each and will get their first real testing today. The Bonanza really looks different with those huge teardrop tanks at the end of each wing. The HF radio antenna runs from above the cabin to the vertical stabilizer then out to the end of the left wing. She looks like she means business. We get aboard and strap in. Bob is six feet tall and our shoulders touch in the cockpit. It's going to be a cozy trip. We close and secure the cockpit door. "All set?" asks Bob.

"All set — Let's fly!"

Bob starts the Allison. The propeller spins and the jet engine spools up smoothly. We wave good-bye to the small crowd, which includes the FAA person who signed off the tanks.

Bob has filed an instrument flight plan for Midland, Texas, about four hours away. Air Traffic Control clears us by flight plan route to maintain an initial altitude of 4,000 feet. We depart at 10:39 a.m. local time in the rain and climb into heavy clouds. Bob engages the autopilot for a smooth climb to

4,000 as we enter the gray world of the instrument pilot. We follow the radar vectors of the ATC controller and as we are turned eastward away from metropolitan San Diego, are cleared to 11,000 feet. At 9,500 feet we break into brilliant sunshine. We reach our cruising altitude and Bob reduces power to cruise setting. We settle in for the flight. The GPS shows our ground speed at 178 knots. Those big tip-tanks are costing us at least five knots of airspeed. For some of the longer legs later in this trip around the world we will be so heavy at takeoff that our airspeed will be drastically reduced until we burn off much of our fuel.

As we cross the Cuyamaca range we leave the local Pacific storm behind and fly into an area of broken to scattered clouds. We cross the Imperial Valley and the Arizona border. Yuma is behind us and Gila Bend lies ahead. The sky clears.

After two hours the main tanks are down to half full. Bob turns on the pumps that will transfer fuel from the tips to the mains. They feed normally as

*Jack Murphy Stadium visible climbing out of San Diego.*

they replace the fuel being burned by the engine. The transfer is at a slightly higher rate than engine consumption and the main tanks slowly fill up. Everything looks okay. We land at Midland at 4:50 p.m. local time in clear weather. After fueling the plane we take off again at 6:30 p.m. going VFR (Visual Flight Rules) in clear skies with Shreveport, Louisiana in our minds as a destination. We are fugitives running from the violent weather that dominates the center of America. By going this way we are adding hundreds of miles to our trip to Montreal, but it can't be helped.

As darkness falls Bob turns on the cockpit and navigation lights. But wait, the switch for the navigation lights won't stay on. It goes to the "off" position as soon as he takes his finger away. We check the circuit breakers but that is not the problem. It must be a short in the system and there is nothing we can do about it from the cockpit. We will have to land soon or we won't be legal. The nearest large airport is Austin, Texas, and we set course for it. Bonanza 9675 Romeo sets down at Austin in the last light of the day. The aircraft is secured for the night and we head for the local Holiday Inn. The short in the navigation lights will have to wait for later.

**WEDNESDAY, 27 APRIL.** We depart Austin at 8:35 a.m. on an IFR clearance above scattered clouds, and test the tanks further. We'll soon be ready to try them with the maximum load of 50 gallons each. A converted prop-jet Bonanza, for longer range, is normally equipped with small tip-tanks that hold 20 gallons each. Bob has replaced them with these monsters but has kept the same electric transfer pumps used on the smaller tanks. He had his mechanic add another pump and independent electrical circuit to each tank for redundancy purposes should one pump or circuit fail. It would be maddening to have over two hours of fuel in a tank, just seventeen feet away, yet not be able to use it because of a pump or circuit failure.

The weather clears as we head eastward over Louisiana. Bob cancels the ATC clearance and we proceed VFR. I love the southern landscape, all pine trees and green farms. Bob decides to land at Jackson, Mississippi for coffee and a weather check. We arrive at the pretty airport and head for the Flight Service Station at 11:12 a.m. in the morning. The FSS man on duty shows us the latest meteorological maps and forecasts. Our direct route to Montreal from here would be over Tennessee, Kentucky, West Virginia and Pennsylvania, but that region is still afflicted with violent and dangerous thunderstorms.

We fuel and depart at 12:22 local with no particular destination in mind. Our aim is to get as far east and north as possible before sunset (no night flying without lights) while staying clear of the violent weather. We pass over Montgomery, Alabama, and Columbus, Georgia, listening all the while for reports of weather. Huge buildups of clouds loom ahead. The Stormscope shows they are full of electrical energy. We thread our way through the cloud valleys that separate the boiling towers of rising water vapor as they work themselves up to be this afternoon's thunderstorms. Almost trapped in a box canyon of clouds, we divert south to stay clear. We are only about one hundred miles from the Atlantic coast when we finally put the frontal system behind us and fly into clear air. 9675R is turned to the north and at last we are headed in the direction of Montreal. We parallel the front as we enter the airspace of South Carolina and watch the storms on our left mature in the late afternoon. Bob consults his airport directory and decides that Fayetteville, North Carolina will be our destination for today. We land at 5:04 p.m. local time and seek out a motel for the night. If the weather is good tomorrow, we will try for Montreal nonstop — 742 nautical miles away.

**THURSDAY, 28 APRIL.** The day turns out to be perfect. The front has passed out to sea during the night and left behind clear skies. The weather looks good all the way north. The Bonanza is fueled with a near-full fuel load and Bob files an instrument flight plan to Montreal, requesting 9,000 feet cruising altitude. The wheels come up at 8:30 a.m. Normal max gross weight on the Bonanza is 3,680 pounds. We are slightly over 4,500 pounds and the takeoff is long and the climb is much slower than usual.

Ninety minutes after takeoff we are approaching Norfolk, Virginia. Visibility is unlimited. I make out the Naval Shipyard at Portsmouth, the entrance to Chesapeake Bay, and the Naval Air Station. We fly up the Delmarva Peninsula, cross Delaware Bay, and are soon over the marshes (they call them "meadows") and farms of southern New Jersey. I lived hereabouts in the 1970s and by following familiar

*A portion of downtown Montreal.*

highways and turnpikes with my eyes I soon spot my old town of Medford Lakes. Thirty miles to our right we can see Atlantic City and the ocean beyond. To the left we can make out the Delaware River and the tall buildings of downtown Philadelphia. What a day! This is what flying is all about.

Bob is told to contact New York Center. When he raises them they ask us if we want to remain at 9,000 feet or if we will accept a new altitude of 5,000. Bob is wise in the ways of controllers around New York City. He knows if we remain high we will be routed away from the area, sent out to sea, and brought around the far east end of Long Island to keep us from cluttering up the approach corridors. He accepts clearance to 5,000 and we are radar vectored directly toward the heart of the city. Staten Island is below us, then the Lower Bay. There's Coney Island! To our left the skyscrapers of lower Manhattan, dominated by the World Trade Center towers, stand out clearly in the sunshine. We are brought smack over JFK Airport at 5,000 feet. The whole city looks like a scale model of itself except the cars, buses, trucks and people are actually moving around. North of JFK we are vectored across Queens then north by northwest over the Bronx. We rejoin airways north of the city and are cleared back to 9,000 feet as we follow the Hudson River upstream. What a way to tour New York! We have seen more sights in twenty minutes than Grayline could show us in a week.

One by one the cities of the Hudson Valley pass.

Poughkeepsie, Albany, Sarasota Springs. Lake Champlain appears to our right. As we get nearer to the Canadian border, scattered, then broken clouds appear. Turbulence begins to rock the aircraft as we are handed off to Montreal Center. We start a descent and are switched to Montreal Approach Control. Over the St. Lawrence River we get a good shaking up in the turbulence as we are vectored to the approach to St. Hubert Airport. We land at St. Hubert at 1:24 p.m. local time. The flight has taken four hours, fifty-four minutes. The entire fuel system has operated perfectly. No more testing is needed.

The tower directs us to a concrete pad in front of a relocatable structure flying the Canadian Maple Leaf. It is, of course, Customs and Immigration. Bob shuts down and we go inside. The Bonanza's jet engine must cool down for ten or fifteen minutes before a restart is attempted so we are in no hurry. The uniformed inspector on duty processes us in a few minutes and we hang around inside, out of the chilly wind that blows across the airfield. I start chatting with the Customs official, a pleasant middle-aged man, and as soon as I mention that I am a retired federal employee of the US, he gives me an earful on the arbitrary nature of Canadian bureaucratic management, their paltry pension system, stingy resource allocations, and the usual litany of grievances you would get from almost any lower level civil servant. I conclude there is not a lot of difference on either side of the border.

We climb in the plane, fire up and roll over to Aerotaxi, a repair and fueling facility where all the racers are to assemble. We are a day early and only a few of the other racers have arrived. Meeting us is Bryant Quantz, owner of Aerotaxi, who greets us warmly in his French Canadian way and sees to our every need. As soon as we mention the inoperable navigation lights he clears space in one of his hangars, pushes 75R inside, and assigns a mechanic to the problem. In fifteen minutes the mechanic finds a reversed polarity connection to the starboard green wing light, rewires and tests it, and we are back to one hundred percent airworthiness. The Bonanza is fueled, in liters, and tied down on the ramp.

We hitch a ride to downtown Montreal to the Queen Elizabeth Hotel where all racers and officials are quartered. At the hotel we run into another fel-

*Racer "Spirit of Pacific" N911WT, an A36 Beechcraft Bonanza owned by Dr. Wilfred Tashima.*

*Right and below:*

*Racer "Tiger" Cessna Conquest N1210U, owned by Vijaypat Singhania from India. It is orange with black stripes, the most striking paint design of any of the racers.*

low racer and old friend from the 1992 World Air Rally, Dr. Wilfred Tashima. Dr. Willie is a general surgeon from Honolulu and an all-around good guy. He's about sixty years old, but could pass for forty. He has acquired a Bonanza like Bob's since we last saw him, but kept the stock powerplant and has rigged the plane with the large *Dolly Parton* tip-tanks just like Bob's. His plane is slower than ours but can stay in the air for eighteen hours or more. Willie flew the airplane, alone, from Honolulu to California. Once there he picked up his new flying partner, Herb Halperin, whom we now meet.

Herb is a semi-retired aeronautical engineer and private pilot from Los Angeles. He's in his early seventies. He and Dr. Willie got together through an ad Willie had placed in several aviation publications seeking a flying partner for the World Air Race and someone to share expenses. Herb is a real talker and as the four of us have dinner, regales and charms us with many a story.

FRIDAY, 28 APRIL. Bob and I spend a lazy morning. The Queen Elizabeth Hotel is right downtown in Montreal so we take a stroll to the old part of the city. It is an overcast and dull day. We visit a cathedral where Bob, a lifelong Catholic, prays for a safe journey. At 12:15 p.m. Aerotaxi sends a van for us and we are taken back to St. Hubert's airfield where it has been arranged for Bob to give an interview for Canadian TV. Bernard Lamy is a publicity hound and throughout the race we will find that he never misses a chance to hold a press conference or seek television coverage. What the hell, it's a newsworthy event, isn't it? We are always happy to oblige if it promotes general aviation.

At the airport Bob stands by his plane and talks to a reporter for a few minutes in front of the cameras. If this segment ever airs on local television we will both miss it. Afterward, Bob has the Bonanza's oxygen bottle topped off. Neither of us can

The list of the entrants is as follows:

*Piston (Normal aspirated)*

| | | |
|---|---|---|
| Bonanza (A36) N911WT *Spirit of Pacific* | Wilfred Tashima Herbert Halperin | USA |
| Twin Commanche N33226 *Tail Wind World Flyer* | Marion Jayne Patricia Keefer | USA |
| Glasair III N640KJ *Zephyrus* | Ken Johnson Larry Cioppi | USA |
| B58 Baron N8282U *Cumulus Bound* | Arthur Mott Thomas Hatch | USA |

*Piston (Turbocharged)*

| | | |
|---|---|---|
| Cessna 210 N5531W *Go Johny Go* | Erik Banck Merce Inglada | Belgium Spain |
| Cessna 421B CGDPL *Kona Wind* | Dawn Bartsch Gordon Bartsch | Canada |
| Cessna 340 VH-HMN *Spirit of 76* | Margaret Ringenberg Adele Foggle Daphne Schiff | USA Canada Canada |
| Cessna 210 N731MT *Norway* | Poju Stephansen Jan Roang | Norway |
| Piper Navajo Panther N719PS *Empty Pockets Express* | David Sherrill Nancy Law | USA |
| Mooney 252 (M20K) F-GHBJ *Baccarat* | Jean Balthazard Claude Guenette | France |
| Merlin N300AL *LA-Z-BOY* | Harlon Hain Chuck Forcey | USA |

*Turboprops*

| | | |
|---|---|---|
| Cessna Conquest N792KC *Oak Lawn Express* | Kenneth Lindstrom Carol Lindstrom | USA |
| Cheyenne I HB-LLK *Hors Ligne* | Bruno Keppeler Nicholas Poncet | Swiss |
| Bonanza Turbine N9675R *Spirit of San Diego* | Robert Reiss Dennis Stewart | USA |
| Cessna Conquest N1210U *Tiger* | Vijaypat Singhania Daniel Brown Peter Troy-Davies | India USA UK |

*Organization Aircraft*

| | | |
|---|---|---|
| Super King Air F-GILU *Arc en Ciel I* | Bernard Lamy Jeff Bennett Hubert Rault | France USA |
| Citation Jet N525KN *Arc en Ciel II* | Jim Knuppe Mike Wilson | USA |
| Citation II HB-VBM *Arc en Ciel III* | Jean Claude Kaufman Marcel Hurschler Anne Lene Odegaard-Emmanouil | Swiss |

*Chase Aircraft*

| | | |
|---|---|---|
| Citation II N136BC *Arc en Ciel IV* | Dhananjay Gole Narenda Srivatava Jo Kendrick Venetia Simcock | India |

think of anything else to do to get the airplane ready.

By afternoon most of the racers have assembled and we begin to get acquainted with some of them. The most striking aircraft of the group is a Cessna Conquest from India. The large twin turboprop aircraft is painted bright orange and covered with tiger stripes. It has fierce eyes and a mouth painted on its nose. It attracts crowds just standing there. Alongside of this dramatic aircraft is a Citation II jet in plain coloring whose function will be to fly chase carrying spare parts, mechanics, and relief pilots for the one in tiger stripes. This elaborate and costly lashup is owned and supervised by one Vijaypat Singhania, Indian industrial titan (textile mills, etc.) and as we will soon find out, a most serious competitor.

That evening Bernard Lamy hosts a dinner for all the racers in a private room at the Queen Elizabeth. Speeches are made. Tomorrow we must all go to the airport and pass our final test before the race begins.

SATURDAY, 30 APRIL. All crews are assembled at St. Hubert's field. Officials of the Canadian Ministry of Transport are there to check all aircraft for proper certification and survival equipment before they are cleared to fly the North Atlantic. No one can object to this since it is the Canadian Government's responsibility to find you and fish you out if you go down out there.

All aircraft must have this minimum equipment:

— Two automatic direction finder (ADF) receivers; or one ADF and one Global Positioning System receiver.
— High Frequency radio.
— Life raft and rations.
— Emergency Landing Transmitter (ELT), salt water activated.
— Emergency signal light, waterproof.
— Sufficient fuel capacity for estimated time en route plus three hours reserve.
— If the aircraft is single-engine, each crew member must have a floatable rubber immersion suit.

Two teams of officials perform the examinations and it is all over in two hours. Bob's aircraft gets through smoothly. He had faxed copies of all the fuel tank modification documents before we left San Diego and the Canadians are well pleased with their completeness.

Aerotaxi has cleared out their main hangar and a big luncheon and press conference are held. Each of us is presented with an official jacket with the race logo, an FAI patch, and velcro strips on the breast where we can place the names of the various race sponsors as we pass from country to country.

A French Canadian folk music band saws away on a platform at the rear of the hangar in front of a large map showing the entire course of the race. Rain pours down outside and it is windy and cold. So much for spring in Quebec. The race starts tomorrow morning and the weather forecast is lousy.

The group dinner that night has a serious air about it. Voices are subdued as

*Musicians play at the Montreal luncheon in front of a map of the race route.*

good luck toasts are proposed. The Indian team, with Vijaypat at its center, holds a long discussion in a corner of the room. We break up early and get to bed. Tomorrow we head for St. John's, on the very eastern tip of Newfoundland.

Following are thumbnail sketches of some of the other race teams:

Twin Commanche N33226   Marion Jayne
*Tail Wind World Flyer*      Patricia Keefer

Marion and Pat are a mother-daughter team from the Dallas area. Marion has been an avid flyer most of her adult life and has many thousands of hours. Their combined good looks and winning charms dull many of the others at first to the fact that they are both superb pilots and fierce competitors. In the days ahead they will push their Commanche to its design limits and a bit beyond.

B58 Baron N8282U       Arthur Mott
*Cumulus Bound*         Thomas Hatch

Arthur is a man in his 60s from New Jersey. He is a high time pilot and flight instructor. Money does not seem to be one of his problems. His copilot, Thomas Hatch, is 28 and an experienced pilot himself. Arthur has bought a brand new B58 Baron for this race and has equipped it with enormous internal gasoline tanks for additional range.

Cessna 210 N5531W      Erik Banck
*Go Johny Go*          Merce Inglada

Erik is a Swede, living in Belgium, who is in the computer business. His English is very good. Mustachioed and given to goofy looking hats, he goes around with a small cigar in his mouth at all times, almost defying any non-smoker to ask him to put it out. His copilot, Merce, is a young and cute flying instructor from Spain. She loves to party. Her English is marginal at best on the ground. Put her on the radio in the air and she can achieve almost pure incoherence. I have no idea how these two got together. Erik is determined to win his class and is quite open about it. I suspect he is cutting a lot of air traffic control corners while in the air. That's all right with the race rules as long as you don't get caught.

Navajo Panther N719P       David Sherrill
*Empty Pockets Express*      Nancy Law

This handsome couple from Maryland are relatively young in age among the racers. They seem new to long-distance flying and somewhat inexperienced, but both are very game. Their aircraft will be constantly plagued by problems, one of the most serious will be an inoperative heater which can be serious at the 20,000 plus feet altitudes at which they usually fly.

Cessna 340 VH-HMN   Margaret Ringenberg
*Spirit of 76*            Adele Foggle
                      Daphne Schiff

This trio of ladies are to win the admiration of the entire group for their determination and professionalism. All three are members of the 99's, the

*Racer "Tail Wind World Flyer" Twin commanche N33226.  Crew:  Marion Jayne and Patricia Keefer*

*Left:*

*Racer "Empty Pockets Express," a Piper Navajo Panther N719P with David Sherrill and Nancy Law as crew.*

*Right:*

*Racing participant Margaret Ringenberg speaks to television cameras in Montreal with the "Spirit of 76," a Cessna 340 VH-HMN in the background. Adele Foggle and Daphne Schiff completed this three-women crew.*

*Racer "Norway," a Cessna 210 N731MT with Poju Stephansen and Jan Roang as crew.*

women's organization whose purpose is to promote and expand women's role in aviation. Margaret is from Indiana where she is something of a legend for her accomplishments in aviation as an instructor and flyer. She is in her mid-70s. Adele and Daphne are two Canadians who both teach at the college level in aviation subjects. The aircraft they originally intended to enter in this race broke down at the last minute and the Canadian-registered Cessna 340 they are flying was a last-minute replacement. It is not the best type for a course like this because it doesn't have enough range. They know they cannot compete well but have come along for the challenge and excitement of being part of the event.

Cessna 210 N731MT          Poju Stephansen
*Norway*                   Jan Roang

Poju and Jan, each in his 40s, are both square-shooter types who are also serious competitors. Both are fluent in English, and Jan, especially, seems highly expert on the Cessna 210 and its sys-

tems. Like many other Europeans they find it more convenient and economical to keep their aircraft registered in the USA, even to the point of flying a mechanic from the US to Norway once a year to perform the required annual inspection (most European nations seem to have some kind of bureaucratic vendetta against general aviation). Both of them are in this to win and their most serious competition within their class, Erik Banck, seems to irritate them with both his manner and methods.

Cessna Conquest N792KC   Kenneth Lindstrom
*Oak Lawn Express*        Carol Lindstrom

This couple from Oak Lawn, Illinois, a suburb of Chicago, are the only serious competition for Vijay Singhania in the Turboprop class. Both Ken and Carol are in their 50s. Ken is in the contracting business. Carol seems a bit superstitious and prone to see omens in casual remarks or events. They are a very pleasant couple and good company.

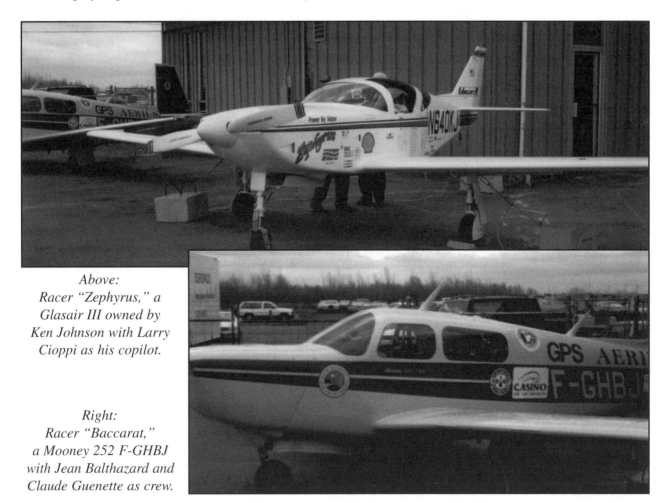

*Above:*
*Racer "Zephyrus," a Glasair III owned by Ken Johnson with Larry Cioppi as his copilot.*

*Right:*
*Racer "Baccarat," a Mooney 252 F-GHBJ with Jean Balthazard and Claude Guenette as crew.*

## FLASHBACK II

## "THE LONELINESS OF COMMAND"

NOVEMBER 1954. It was a beautiful day in central Oklahoma. Visibility was at least fifty miles in cobalt skies. Five thousand feet over the fields and farms a T-28A "Trojan" belonging to the Air Training Command at Vance AFB was flying southward. Aboard were two Aviation Cadets. Sid Wayne of New York City was in the forward seat at the controls. Our hero sat in the rear seat waiting his turn to fly the plane.

The two were not strictly legal at this point. By regulation they were supposed to stay within the large Vance practice area at all times. But today, with no instructor aboard, they had impulsively decided to take a look at Oklahoma City.

The Cadet in the rear seat gazed around the cockpit. On a whim he decided to screw up old Sid a little. He reached down and spun the rudder trim all the way to the left and the elevator trim down, then waited to see what Sid would do.

The T-28 went into a shallow left descent and began a wide uncoordinated spiral toward the earth. As they passed through 2,000 feet both Cadets became aware they were getting close to the giant TV tower north of the city. At 1,200 feet our hero saw something flash beneath the right wing.

"Hey Sid, be careful! You just missed one of the guy wires for the TV tower by about fifty feet!"

"Wha d'ya mean me? You're flying the plane!"

When the trim controls had changed suddenly and the control stick had jerked in Sid's hand he had assumed his buddy in the rear seat was signaling for control of the aircraft. He also assumed the engine noise had drowned out the usual "I got it" on the interphone and had taken his hands and feet away from the controls.

No one had been flying the T-28 for over ten minutes.

# CHAPTER 3

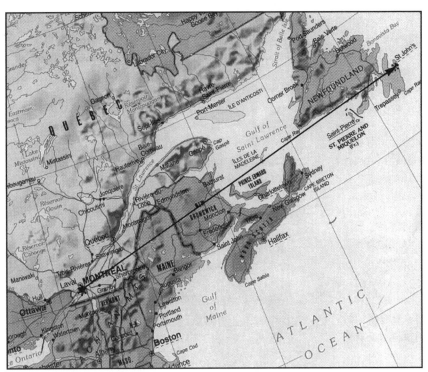

# MONTREAL

# TO

# ST. JOHN'S

SUNDAY, 1 MAY 1994. At 7:00 a.m. all are assembled at St. Hubert's for the weather briefing. The Canadian officials are really good at this sort of thing — very professional. Outside it is raining and cold, and the crew members are wearing parkas and heavy rain gear. There is a big front just off Montreal with heavy clouds and low ceilings forecast for halfway to St. John's. Freezing levels are at 3,000 feet in clouds. Like everyone else, we have filed an IFR (Instrument Flight Rules) plan with ATC for the shortest route to St. John's which is due east from Montreal on V352 Houlton, V471 Moncton, V300 Sidney, and V312 to Torbay. But on the first half of that route the airway minimum altitudes run as high as 7,800 feet. Bob and I quickly study our alternatives. Icing is the one thing that really worries us. The Bonanza has a heated propeller and a heated air intake for the jet engine, but nothing beyond that. We'll be heavy at takeoff — St. John's is almost 900 nautical miles from here — and we won't be able to carry much ice. Maybe there's another way we can

go. To the north the weather looks a little better. We could follow the valley of the St. Lawrence River to Quebec City and then stay at 5,000 feet as the river widens into the Gulf of St. Lawrence. From Natash on the north shore we could cross the gulf to the island of Newfoundland. Bob decides that is the way for us to go. I begin to file a new flight plan but we are advised by the operations people that a last-minute change in the paperwork may lead to confusion and delays. All the racers have a narrow time slot for departure and it will go better if we accept our originally requested clearance, take off, and then immediately ask for a re-routing.

We advise Bernard of our intentions to go this alternate route and that because of the increased distance, we will probably be late getting into St. John's. He is not to worry if we are a bit late. Bernard hears this news with a shrug. As long as we depart on time it's OK with him.

Our scheduled departure time is 10:10 a.m. The piston powered aircraft depart first. From the ramp we can see them taxi out one by one, perform their runups, and then take the active runway. All the months of preparations for the crews and aircraft have come to this, the start of the race. As each begins the takeoff roll the tower will record the time of departure and transmit it ahead to St. John's for the official record. When each plane leaves the runway it disappears quickly into the rain and clouds.

Bob starts the engine and we are cleared to taxi. We receive our clearance.

"Bonanza 9675 Romeo cleared to St. John's via Victor 352 Houlton, flight plan route. Maintain four thousand. After departure turn to heading one three five. Expect clearance to nine thousand five minutes after departure. Squawk one one three two. Contact departure control on 128.6 after takeoff."

Bob reads back the clearance and we are cleared for takeoff. We break ground at 1015 local time and at 400 feet are on instruments. Bob raises departure control.

"N9675R requests clearance to St. John's via direct Quebec, direct Riviere du Loup, Victor 98 Sept Iles, RR2 Natash, direct Deer Lake R16 St. John's at 5,000 feet."

It's as if the departure controller expected it (he's probably been tipped off by the operations people).

He comes back immediately with the requested clearance and we turn north for Quebec City.

We are in solid clouds at 5,000 feet. Both of us check frequently for ice accumulation on the wings, but there is none. The outside temperature at 5,000 feet varies between zero and plus one Centigrade. This goes on for an hour and a half until we are just north of Riviere du Loup when the ceiling raises a bit and we are suddenly in clear weather under a gray canopy of clouds. We're flying over a winter wilderness! The St. Lawrence River is to our right as we expected, but ahead and to the north is a forest void of human habitation still locked in snow and ice. The lakes are frozen over. We left Montreal on a raw spring day but just over 200 miles to the northeast we have flown back into winter!

Because of today's weather my carefully planned and studied route from Montreal to St. John's is useless history. Our last minute change in routing has increased the distance to fly by almost two hundred nautical miles, but we have more than ample fuel to cover that. At the highest point of our swing to the north before heading southeast for St. John's we will fly off my carefully prepared ONC terrain chart and will be left with only the Jeppesen instrument charts for navigation. This, I will find,

*The frozen north between Montreal and St. John's.*

will be a recurring circumstance on the trip as we encounter the vagaries of weather, air traffic control re-routing, and governmental whims. Flexibility is a necessary virtue for the international airman.

We continue on over the frozen land. At 5,000 feet one can see all the details below. A two-lane road runs along the north bank of the river, a thin line that connects the tiny settlements strung out far from each other along the shore. There seems to be no traffic on the road this Sunday. We pass over the town of Sept Iles. How small it is! Just a cluster of a few buildings in all this open space. Sept Iles has a VOR/DME. These Canadian airways are a mixture of Victor airways and non-directional beacons that make up corresponding low frequency airways. Although low frequency airways are almost a thing of the past in the States, I guess many of the bush pilots in these parts still navigate by an ADF needle. GPS receivers are getting cheaper every year and I imagine all these expensive and hard to maintain ground radio aids will someday disappear.

The cloud base is getting lower. Bob requests clearance to descend to 4,000 and receives it. The air traffic controllers are fully bilingual up here. If a pilot calls them in French, they speak French. If another speaks English, they reply in English.

We pass over the few buildings that make up the village of Minigan. Ahead lies Natashquan where we will turn southeast and begin our transit of the Gulf of St. Lawrence. What seemed to start out as a day of bucking nasty weather has turned into a splendid scenic flight in smooth air at low altitude. You never know. We're actually having a good time up here. Bob opens his Stanley thermos bottle and pours himself a cup of hot coffee.

The large island of Anticosti is dimly visible off to our right as the river widens into the Gulf of St. Lawrence proper. At Natash VOR we report our passing and give ATC an estimate for Deer Lake, Newfoundland, 182 nautical miles to the east southeast, and begin our flight over 138 miles of open water. At our low altitude the shore disappears rapidly and soon we can see nothing but steel colored water under a solid overcast of clouds. There's not a lot of wind out here and the Gulf waters are almost smooth.

The auxiliary cabin tank has been drained first and the tip-tanks are now feeding into the mains. I have programmed the GPS receiver for both Deer Lake and St. John's airport. The display window on the instrument has a vertical bar that shows if you are left or right of a direct course to your next objective. It can measure your variance for up to five miles either side of centerline. When over water and out of sight of land, it's a real comfort to know not only the distance to your objective, but also if you are on the right track toward it. Because of our low altitude we won't be able to receive VOR/ADF signals out in the middle of the Gulf so the GPS becomes our primary means of navigation. From time to time I reach over and make small adjustments to the "bug" on the course heading indicator. As I do this the autopilot takes up the new heading and we stay on the centerline of our intended course.

After forty minutes over the water we begin to make out a thin line on the horizon, darker than the Gulf waters. Newfoundland! Closer, the rugged shoreline shows no evidence that this island is populated. No towns, no roads, no telephone lines mark the presence of human beings. Leif Ericsson himself, if alive today, could not see any difference in this land in the seven hundred years since he was here.

We cross the coastline, pass Deer Lake, and begin the last leg of the flight, 207 nautical miles to St. John's, about one hour, thirteen minutes away. Below us it is still winter. The hills are covered in snow and all the lakes are frozen tight. Summers must be damn short up here, although I remember back to 1971 when I was on a Pan American jet from London to New York traveling on Navy business. We stopped to refuel at Gander because of strong headwinds over the Atlantic. Gander is about 100 miles north of St. John's and on that August day the temperature was 92° F in the shade. The Newfoundlanders were on the verge of melting — it was an all-time record high. Well, that's not the case today. Spring is not here yet.

St. John's airport is reporting VFR conditions under a 5,000 foot overcast. As we near the field the town of St. John's appears under our nose. It's a pretty, New England style of city built around a classic deep-water harbor. The houses are blue or white and most are square two-story structures with steep roofs. It must be warmer on this side of the island. The city is free of snow.

N9675R is cleared for a visual approach. There seems to be no other traffic about. Bob gets on the radio and requests permission to circle overhead to take some photographs and is given the okay. The autopilot is disengaged and I fly the aircraft while Bob digs out his Nikon and begins shooting away. I'm doing figure eight's right over the airport at 1,000 feet when we see a commercial Boeing 737 taxi out. The tower asks us politely to knock off the sightseeing and let them get back to business. We enter a downwind leg and come in to land. Arrival is at 5:24 p.m. Elapsed time from Montreal has been five hours, thirty-nine minutes. The total distance flown: 1,021 nautical miles. Average ground speed: 181 knots. I estimate we have at least another three hours of fuel aboard when we land.

We fuel up on the cold and windy ramp and are transported into town in the protracted afternoon of these northern latitudes. The Newfoundland Hotel is a modern multi-storied structure that would be a first-class accommodation in any city. There's a reception for us with the leading citizens present. A plentiful buffet is spread out in the ballroom. After dinner the Mayor of St. John's, a dignified elderly man, welcomes us and reminds us of the important role of St. John's in the early history of flying the Atlantic. When we depart tomorrow morning for the Azores, he tells us, we will be following in the steps of many pioneers.

During May, 1919, exactly seventy-five years ago, St. John's was the focus of the world's attention as four attempts to be the first across the Atlantic were prepared and then tried. On May 16th three US Navy Curtiss flying boats at Trepassy Bay, just a few miles south of here, lifted out of the water and set course for the Azores. Two of them were forced down short of the islands but their crews survived. One, the NC-4 commanded by Lieutenant Commander Albert Read with a crew of six, made the Azores and went on to Portugal and England, reaching Plymouth on May 31st. It was the first crossing of the Atlantic by air and, although a considerable achievement, is not considered a "nonstop crossing" continent to continent because they stopped at the Azores.

Two days after the seaplanes departed Trepassy Bay a large Sopwith biplane, the *Atlantic*, rolled down an improvised runway at St. John's. Harry

*St. John's Airport in Newfoundland.*

28

Hawker and Kenneth MacKenzie-Grieve were attempting to fly to Brooklands, England nonstop. A thousand miles out over the Atlantic their cooling system failed and they ditched in the cold waters next to a passing freighter. Both airmen were rescued. That same day, May 18, 1919, two more intrepid flyers took the runway at St. John's aiming for England. F.P. Raynham and C.W.F. Morgan in the Martinsyde biplane *Raymor* crashed on takeoff and the aircraft was destroyed. A little over three weeks later, on June 14th, Captain John Alcock and Lt. Arthur Whitten Brown, RAF, departed Lester's Field, St. John's, in their Vickers "Vimy" converted WWI bomber. Sixteen hours later they sat down and then nosed over at Clifden Aerodrome, Ireland. They had made the first successful nonstop crossing between the new world and the old, a distance of 1,680 miles.

The Mayor adds a personal recollection of these early days. In June 1928, he was seven years old. A team of flyers were waiting for the weather to improve over the Atlantic before setting out in their floatplane *Friendship* from Trepassy Bay in an attempt to reach Ireland. His father took him to see the plane and there he met the three American crew members: Wilbur Stultz (pilot), Louis Gordon (mechanic) and Amelia Earhart (relief pilot). He shook her hand just two days before she became the first woman to cross the Atlantic by air.

Our group appreciates the hospitality and good wishes of these warm people. The pleasant mood of the evening is shattered shortly thereafter when Bernard Lamy announces that each aircraft must fill out complete ICAO flight plans for the entire Atlantic crossing, St. John's — Azores, and Azores — Marrakech. It must be done tonight, and he wants them in half an hour.

Along with others, I race up to our room, get my navigation bag, and bring it down. On the same tables where we have just had dinner we fill out the ICAO forms. Besides the requested routing and altitude we must include coded information on survival gear aboard, radios, number of crew, coloring of the aircraft, alternate airports, estimates of elapsed time to Flight Information Region boundaries, and fuel aboard. I hate doing things like this under pressure, especially when I know it is not really necessary. As an old center controller myself I know these plans can be filed tomorrow before departure. There's also an almost sure bet that the Azores will not receive the plans anyway and we will have to refile there.* As we hand them to Bernard they are inspected for completeness. I feel like a schoolboy turning in some class assignment. It's easy to build up resentful feelings toward people who are ordering you about. I'll try to keep in mind that Bernard has a tough job keeping this whole effort on track. Pilots in general are not noted for their small egos, and the potential for friction is always high in a group like

*Ken Johnson standing by his Glasair reviewing a few details of the race.*

this. I decide to do my best to be cooperative and keep any smart-ass remarks to myself.

**\*This turned out to be an accurate prediction.**

# FLASHBACK III

## "YOUR TAX DOLLARS AT WORK"

DECEMBER 1954. Two Aviation Cadets were aloft in a twin-engine B-25 "Mitchell" bomber. Our hero was in the left seat steering the aircraft over the frozen plains of Oklahoma. The two were "student solo" meaning there was no instructor aboard. They were up there to build up time and, hopefully, practice some of their newly won flying skills.

The outside air temperature was 28 degrees below zero at 9,000 feet, The temperature inside the cockpit was about the same (no one could ever seem to get a B-25's gasoline powered cockpit heater to work). Both Cadets were bundled in two sets of long underwear, winter flying suits, heavy boots, B-15 flight jackets, gloves and flying helmets. Despite all this they were still cold. They were also bored.

Pressing his throat mike, the pilot said, "Ya know, I was thinking about what you could really do in a Baker two bits. It's a heavy bird, but it's real strong. I'll bet a guy could barrel roll one of these things if he got up enough speed."

The copilot thought about this for a minute, then replied "Bullshit! You can't go around doing stunts in a bomber. See the placard on the panel? It says 'all acrobatic maneuvers prohibited.'"

"Oh yeah? I'll bet you two bucks I can do a barrel roll right now."

"You're on, ace."

Our hero pushed the props up, opened the throttles, and dove the Mitchell until it reached 240 miles an hour. He pulled back on the stiff yoke as he turned 20 degrees to the right and when the nose was well above the horizon, gave it hard left on the rudder and wheel to begin the roll.

Now in those days when it seemed almost everyone smoked, the North American Aviation Company had seen fit not to include any ashtrays in its cockpit design. To correct this blunder crews had devised their own solution by taking small used fruit juice cans and soldering wire hooks to their sides. These were hung about the cockpit at various convenient points and used as ashtrays. The problem was that no one felt the responsibility to empty them. They were always jammed full of cigarette butts and ashes.

As the B-25 reached the top of the roll, the pilot didn't apply enough back pressure on the yoke to keep positive "G's" on the airframe (aerobatics had never been his strong point).

At that instant every juice can in the cockpit emptied its butts and ashes on the two Cadets. Cockpit visibility went to zero instantaneously and the airplane entered an inverted stall. Both engines quit from fuel starvation. Many gyrations later and 5,000 feet lower, the Mitchell recovered straight and level flight.

Later, back on the ground, one Cadet paid the other two dollars.

# CHAPTER 4

# ST. JOHN'S TO MARRAKECH

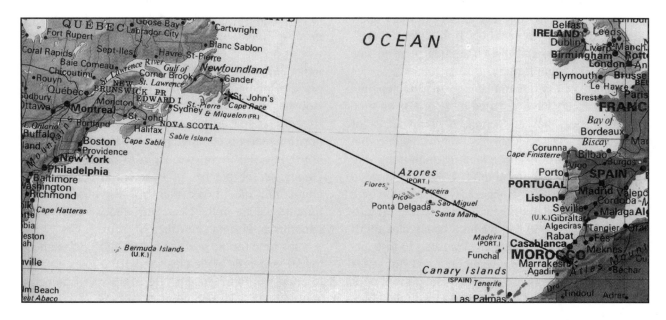

MONDAY, 2 MAY. The day dawns miserably. The front we escaped from in Montreal yesterday has caught up with us again and intensified. By the time we get to St. John's airport freezing rain is falling and the field is below landing minimums for both ceiling and visibility. The wind is blowing hard. When you go outside the operations building for any length of time, your nose begins to run and your ears start to hurt. It is spring weather like this in the Maritime Provinces that was the bane of most early attempts to fly the North Atlantic. Once again Bernard has assigned a takeoff time to each aircraft and ours is 8:15 a.m. Neither Bob nor I like the look of things.

The weather people tell us the heavy clouds will extend halfway to the Azores, but we can expect good weather after that. Winds will be favorable for the entire crossing with 20-25 knots on our tail at 7,000 feet. Bob concentrates on the local weather here at St. John's and its forecast for the next several hours. His concern is that if we depart while it is still below landing minimums and develop a mechanical problem that forces us to abandon the Atlantic crossing, where can we go? Gander is a hundred miles away and experiencing the same weather. We talk it over and Bob decides the prudent thing to do is wait a few hours. The local forecast is for slightly improving conditions.

When Bernard Lamy is informed that we are going to drop out of the departure sequence and wait for the weather to improve, he explodes with Gallic anger.

"You cannot ruin the departure plan. It is all pre-pared. I will not permit it! If you wait it might get worse and you will find yourself flying in the mud all the way to the Azores! You must be bold! If you are timid you should not be a part of this."

Bernard has come within an inch of accusing us of cowardice. Bob makes a visible effort to control himself. He stands up, moves nearer to Lamy, and looks him in the eye. His voice is calm.

"Look, Bernard, You can say anything you like,

but I'm in command of my aircraft, not you, and I'm the one responsible for the safety of myself and my crew, not you. It's my decision to delay my takeoff and there's nothing you can do about it. So leave us alone. This discussion is over."

This brings Lamy up short. You can almost see his mental wheels spinning. He is in charge — yes — but only up to a point. This is not a military operation and he's not a general. Bob's right, there's nothing he can do and there's nothing more to say. He leaves the room fuming.

A little over two hours later we start the engine. The other racers have departed more or less on time and fortunately have experienced no incidents or emergencies. The weather has improved somewhat and St. John's is now above landing minimums. We take off at 10:07 a.m. local time (1237 Zulu), loaded with fuel. Bob lets the Bonanza fly off after the long surface run and starts a gentle climb while the airspeed builds. At 300 feet we hit a strong downdraft and as Bob holds the plane level we start to lose airspeed. Abruptly, we are in an updraft and Bob eases the nose over to regain our speed. He is handling it just right, nothing but easy movements on the yoke. At these weights every flight is a test flight and any violent maneuver could be our last. We pass through the rough air and enter solid clouds.

Lajes, in the Azores, lies 1,244 nautical miles to the southeast. There is no place to land between here and there. We have filed, and been cleared on, a flight plan that looks like this:

CYYT (St. John's) direct N47W050 direct N46W045 direct N45W040 (Santa Maria Oceanic FIR) direct N43W035 direct OSCAR direct NOVEMBER direct LPLA (Lajes) FL70 (Flight level 7,000 feet with altimeter at 29.92 inches). Alternate: LPAZ (Santa Maria, Azores). ETE (Estimated time en route): Six hours, three minutes.

I have pre-programmed all these checkpoints, including our destination, into the GPS and now it is simply a matter of following the course indicator and making the required position reports and estimates.

There is no ice in these solid clouds at 7,000 feet — Bueno! That's one thing not to worry about.

Our first checkpoint is coming up. My estimate for N47W050 was 1318Z and we hit it on the nose. My estimate for N46W045 is 1419Z and we hit this one right on the minute also. Bob gives me a funny look as if to say, "How in hell did you do that?" I

make a modest shrug and smile. Let him believe in me as the Master Navigator as long as he can.

Two hours out from St. John's and we are still in clouds. We haven't seen a thing so far. Bob is working on the HF radio. At the time of the second position report he could not make contact with Gander Radio despite repeated attempts. All we can get out of it are some squawks and occasional keyed code groups. Bob bought the radio set from a representative of Arc en Ciel and it looks like he got a piece of junk. We have the VHF frequency for plane-to-plane communication for this part of the Atlantic and Bob has relayed the last position report through a friendly jet airliner somewhere overhead. Our third position report is coming up soon when, almost three hours into the flight, we begin to break out of the clouds. I see patches of blue ocean below. The clouds thin out. Look, there's a freighter! Within minutes we are in the clear, surrounded by scattered cumulus and bright sunshine.

It's time for the position report. Bob gives up on the HF and calls in the clear on VHF for any aircraft to come up on frequency. He is answered immediately by a very British voice.

"November 9675 Romeo, this is Air Caribbean Charter 4733. Can we be of assistance?"

"Roger, Air Caribbean, could you relay a position report for us to Santa Maria?"

"Delighted to help, old man. Go ahead."

"November 9675 Romeo, North 45 West 040 at 1519 Zulu, Flight Level 70; estimating North 43 West 035 at 1629 Zulu, OSCAR next."

The jet overhead reads it back verbatim and then goes off frequency for a minute.

"Air Caribbean here, 75 Romeo, your position report has been received."

"Thank you very much."

"75 Romeo, may I ask what kind of aircraft you are and what you are doing out here?"

"We're a single-engine Beechcraft Bonanza from St. John's, Newfoundland to Lajes in the Azores on a flight around the world." This is received in silence for a few moments.

"Tell me, sir, what does your wife think of this?"

"She tells me she thinks I'm crazy." Another pause.

"Frankly, I tend to agree with her. Good luck, 75 Romeo."

"Thank you, sir."

The weather improves and soon we are in clear skies. Thirty miles to the south I see a broken deck of stratus at about 6,000 feet but we will stay clear of it. Our next position report is again relayed through a friendly jet flying above. We approach intersection OSCAR, located at N41W030. Off to our right, about 60 miles away, looms a volcanic cone sticking up through the stratus layer. It's an eerie sight out here in the middle of the Atlantic, but it is solid land and that's a good sign.

We pass OSCAR and set course for intersection NOVEMBER which marks the boundary of the Azores terminal control area. In a while Bob is talking to Lajes Control and we are radar identified, vectored toward the Lajes airport, and cleared to enter a VFR pattern for landing. It's a huge military field with 12,000 feet of runway. Touchdown is at 6:34 p.m. (1834 Zulu) for six hours, six minutes en route. We are directed to taxi to the Customs area.

There is no sign of the other racers. All the piston aircraft have gone to Santa Maria, about 120 miles east of here, for gasoline, while the turboprops, most of whom departed two hours ahead of us at St. John's, have been here, fueled up with their race clocks running, and have long since departed for Morocco.

A Portuguese Customs official greets us on the ramp. He stamps our passports and collects an airport fee of $47. He is cooperative in arranging for a jet fuel truck and we fill up the Bonanza. Payment for the fuel must be made at the airport Operations building on the other side of the airport, and a car and driver are called to take us there.

I know that during World War II the Portuguese, after considerable Allied arm-twisting, gave the British and Americans permission to establish an air base here at Lajes even though Portugal was officially neutral. For many years after the war this remained an important logistic base for transatlantic fliers. I'm somewhat surprised to see it is still a joint use base. There are several C-5 "Galaxy" and C-141 "Starlifter" transports parked on the ramp.

Once we are in the Operations building and Bob has paid the fuel bill, we are approached by a young Portuguese civilian who offers to be of service while we are here. His name is Elario. He's in his mid-twenties, and has the dark good looks of a matador. His English is only fair. We accept his offer and tell him we are hungry. Would he join us for dinner?

But of course. He has a car, and soon we are climbing to the highest point on the hilly base. It's the US Air Force Officers' Club. When we enter, the headwaiter immediately comes over smiling and snapping his fingers at busboys to prepare a table for three. We're getting the VIP treatment and I can't figure out why. It turns out that Elario, although only a minor functionary in operations, is the eldest son of the Officers' Club manager and thereby rates top service. Elario talks about his life on the islands. He was born and reared here on the base. Understandably, he is a bit rock happy and feels hemmed in on these tiny islands in the ocean. He longs for the bright lights of Lisbon and the world beyond. He envies us, the two world travelers with the magic airplane.

Well, the two world travelers had better haul ass. There's no rest this side of Marrakech. The sun is going down and we have another six hours of night flying ahead of us. We thank Elario for his company and head back to Base Operations for a weather briefing.

The USAF Airman on duty asks us if we are going high or low. The winds look pretty good at 11,000 feet, so we will stay off oxygen. There's some upper level electrical disturbances near the African coast but it shouldn't bother us. My planned route is not a straight line between here and Marrakech, but a course designed to keep us over solid land as much as possible in case of trouble. I file for direct Santa Maria in the Azores, then to Porto Santo in the Madeira Islands and from there a straight course to Casablanca. From Casablanca it is 80 miles due south on airways to Marrakech. It's a little longer this way but, I figure, safer. We taxi out for takeoff.

Back in Montreal we were warned that no aircraft could depart the Azores without a working HF radio. This has worried me a little since that is exactly what we don't have. No one has asked us about it, however, and the tower has not requested a radio check on HF frequencies. Our departure is held up for the approach and landing of a C-5 "Galaxy." What an awesome sight it is as it comes practically right over us, crossing the threshold of the runway. Its navigation, landing, and gear lights all lit up make it look like a flying ocean liner. With the C-5 safely down we are cleared for takeoff at 2132 local and Zulu times. The sun has set and we climb out in the last of the twilight.

Lajes departure control vectors us through their terminal area and we are soon on course, climbing to 11,000 feet, on our way to Santa Maria. It grows fully dark. There is a high layer of clouds above that shuts out the stars. The moon will not rise for us tonight. So here we are, blind to everything but the instruments in our cockpit, glowing amber in our faces, and setting out to cross over eleven hundred nautical miles of mostly water, to a place neither of us has been. This is where preplanning pays off. Navigation now becomes an abstract exercise without reference to anything outside the cockpit. I tune the ADF receiver for the Santa Maria station. When the needle swings 180 degrees showing passage we will change to the predetermined course for FOX-TROT TWO, an intersection at the southeast border of the Azores terminal control area located at 36 degrees, 27 minutes north, and 23 degrees, 54 minutes west.

As we pass each compulsory reporting point I turn on the overhead cockpit light and jot down the position report and estimate for the next route point. Bob then gets on the radio and reads the report to air traffic control. The white overhead light ruins whatever night vision we have built up since the last report but there's nothing to see out there anyway. It's too awkward to fumble around with a flashlight.

Santa Maria is a scattering of lights below us as we pass overhead. 494 nautical miles later the same is true for Porto Santo in the Madeiras. Now we must cross 380 miles of open ocean to the African coast.

Something's going on out there! Through the static on the radio we can faintly hear someone reporting lightning all around and requesting an immediate change to a lower altitude. The rest of the exchange is lost in the static. We will learn later that the call came from Dave Sherrill and Nancy Law in their Navajo Panther. Nearing the African coast at 23,000 feet they have run into that rare aerial phenomenon, sheet lightning. Bouncing between clouds were tremendous discharges of electrical energy that lit up the black skies and seemed to threaten to engulf the entire aircraft. They manage to escape unhurt.

We report LUPEX intersection at 0146Z to Casablanca Center with the help of Caledonia Airlines flight 473 who relays it for us. At AMETA intersection, 80 miles from the coast, we are talking directly to Casablanca Center who now have us on radar. They ask us if we will accept clearance from our present position direct to Marrakech. You bet! That will save us about 55 miles. I set the GPS for Marrakech airport and we turn southeast.

I begin looking for the coastline. When I was flying in the Air Force I made many a landfall at night over a strange coast. Always, in Asia anyway, you could see it a long way off in clear weather because the fishing villages and towns along the shore form a sort of connect-the-dots outline that is unmistakable. Not so here. All is dark ahead. The GPS tells me we are passing from sea to land but I can't see even one small light anywhere. Maybe they don't have electricity down there. It's after two in the morning. Maybe they have simply turned everything off.

We are off airways as we head directly for Marrakech. The controller clears us to descend and maintain 7,000 feet. I unfold my ONC terrain chart for this part of the world and quickly scan for surface elevations. I know that east and south of Marrakech the Atlas Mountains rise to over 13,000 feet. The invisible terrain below us is rugged with hills, but the chart shows none exceeds 4,000 feet. We should be okay. We are given a new altimeter setting in millibars, not inches, of mercury. We have a conversion chart just made for this sort of thing and reset the altimeter to the local pressure.

At fifty miles out from Marrakech we pick up the VOR/DME signal of their local navigation aid.

"November 9675 Romeo. Report fifteen miles out or city lights in sight — whichever comes first."

What? Bob and I look at each other in puzzlement. Marrakech is a big city. We ought to be able to see the glow of their lights on the horizon right now, from fifty miles out. What does he mean, fifteen miles? We fly on.

We are given a descent to 5,000 feet and are reassured that the land is flat because we can see a star or two on the horizon dead ahead. At twenty-five miles the city is still invisible. I'm starting to get concerned. At seventeen miles from the airport a faint yellow glow begins to appear in front of us.

Can that be it? It's like no city I've ever seen before from an airplane at night. As we get closer I begin to see the outlines of streets and broad avenues, but the lights are so far apart, and they glow

*The terminal at Marrakech, Morocco.*

with such a dim amber color, like fifteen-watt bulbs. Whole sections of the city are not lighted at all.

We report fifteen miles out and are switched to the tower. A young-sounding voice, with accented English, clears us for a visual approach to runway 34. Fine, but we have to find the airport first. Neither of us can spot a rotating beacon anywhere. Often you can find a large airport at night by locating a big dark area surrounded by street lights and industrial parks, but not here. We follow the GPS until it tells us we are almost on top of the runway. There! The familiar outline of runway boundary lights and taxiways are below. Bob breaks right and calls us entering the downwind leg. Seven minutes later we are on the ground. The landing was at 0335 local and Zulu time. Six hours, three minutes from the Azores. We departed Canada almost exactly fifteen hours ago.

Ours is the only aircraft moving on this large airport. We turn off the runway where instructed and taxi toward the terminal building. The control tower is visible atop the terminal.

"November 75 Romeo, when you get to the end of the taxiway, turn left for parking."

"75 Romeo, roger."

There's a slight pause. "That's to your left, not mine."

This sets both of us to laughing in the cockpit.

A man with a flashlight directs us to a parking spot among the rest of the race planes which are now all secured for the night. It is obvious that we are the last ones in. As I get out of the cockpit and stretch I am fully aware that I am in Africa for the first time in my life. Different parts of the world have different smells to them, and Africa smells old. People have been living here for a long time. Somewhere near the airport a loudspeaker system is blasting out a muezzin's singsong chants. It sounds like a call to prayer, but at 3:30 in the morning?

The individual who directed our parking now wants our aircraft pushed back to the next parking row. He lends a hand, pushing gently with two fingers on the leading edge of the wing while Bob and I put our backs into it. This pudgy citizen is in a double-breasted suit and when the plane is parked where he wants, he turns to me and states he expects to be paid for his assistance. I give him a dollar but he doesn't seem satisfied. We secure the aircraft, collect our bags, and our new friend directs us to Customs and Immigration. As we enter the terminal he sprints ahead and takes up position behind a counter. It seems he *is* Customs and Immigration in this otherwise empty terminal. He stamps our passports and collects our general Customs declaration. When he is finished he smiles and in broken English states how much he admires the pen in Bob's pocket.

"What did he just say?"

"I think he wants your ballpoint," I whisper.

"I don't understand."

The Moroccan official restates his admiration for the pen and how much he would like to have one just like it. Bob pretends again that he can't understand, but thanks him for his services anyway. The Moroccan is visibly put off by this. My bladder is full after the long flight and I ask for directions to the nearest men's room. The official tells me it is closed and cannot be used tonight, thereby taking his revenge on these two tight-fisted foreigners.

We go around to the front of the terminal and there find a taxi waiting for us. The driver knows our names. Bernard Lamy had promised to provide all ground transportation for the crews and he is coming

through on his word. The driver has already been paid. We ride to the Hotel Imperial Bordj where I finally find a restroom off the lobby. It's nearing five in the morning when we get to our room.

TUESDAY, 3 MAY. "All right, Dennis. Up and at 'em."

"What?" My mind slowly rises to consciousness. Bob is shaking my shoulder.

"C'mon, we've overslept. It's afternoon already. Time to get going."

This doesn't seem right. I'm still exhausted and feel I've only been in bed a few hours. I look at my watch, which I set to local time in the Azores (the Azores and Morocco are in the same time zone). "Goddamn it, Bob! We just checked in here two hours ago. It's only seven thirty in the morning." The brilliant African sunlight is streaming through the curtains.

This gives Bob pause. He studies his watch some more. "Oh. I guess my watch is still on San

*Beautiful and picturesque Marrakech, a memorable oasis in the desert.*

*The "Zephyrus," whose crew had such an alarming experience en route to Marrakech.*

Diego time." Bob does this when he is traveling. He likes to call his wife, Claire, daily when he is away and this is his way of knowing when to call. We are now seven hours ahead of San Diego and it is thirty minutes after midnight there.

"Sorry about that."

I am awake now so I get dressed and we go downstairs for breakfast. The Imperial Bordj is a first-class hotel. There is a European style buffet of breakfast goodies which we share with some of the other racers who are astir this morning.

Ken Johnson, an auto body shop owner about forty years old, tells us of a strange occurrence over the Atlantic yesterday. He flies a beautiful Glasair III, named *Zephyrus*, which he built himself. This small but very fast aircraft won first prize at Oshkosh last year in the Experimental Aircraft Association's homebuilt category. Ken is as tall as I (6'4") and I can't imagine how he fits in that tiny cockpit for hours on end. Anyway, he and his copilot, Larry Cioppi, were tooling along over the Atlantic at 18,000 feet, when they ran into an area of intense electrical activity in the atmosphere. There was no lightning, but they could smell ozone and feel the charged air around them. Suddenly, Larry lit up with St. Elmo's Fire like an incandescent bulb. It had come up their HF trailing antenna. His headset sounded as if angry wasps had invaded his skull. He ripped off the headset and in doing so touched Ken's shoulder, burning a small hole in Ken's flying suit. The whole thing ended an instant later, leaving both men badly shaken but unharmed. An inventory of their avionics revealed that some of the equipment in the aircraft that contained microchips was inoperative. The autopilot was out and so was the transponder, their tiny electronic brains fried by the discharge. Ken and Larry will attempt repairs today.

After breakfast, I return to our room and do a complete hand laundry of shirts, socks and shorts. Laundry is one thing you've got to stay ahead of on a trip like this.

Lunch is served, buffet style again, on the hotel's pool deck. The weather is soft and warm, just like southern California at this time of year. We share a

*The pool and elegant patio reception area at the Hotel Imperial Bordj in Marrakech.*

*More of the city of Marrakech.*

table with the Bartschs. Gordon and Dawn are old flying pals of ours from the 1992 Around the World Air Rally. Both are skilled pilots with many thousands of hours each from the time they ran an air service in Canada's Northwest Territories. It's good to have them along, not only as friends, but because both have proved to be people you can count on for help and advice in any situation. In 1992 their generosity with the store of spare parts they carry in their Cessna 421 saved at least two crews from total breakdown and delay.

After lunch I take a much needed nap. Later, Bob and I decide to take a walk and see some of Marrakech. This proves to be impossible. As soon as we set foot outside the hotel door we are jumped by a swarm of Moroccan shills, all shouting at us, who want to take us to their shops where bargains of unbelievable value can be obtained in rugs, metalware, and inlaid wood furniture. One of them is eager to guide us to the local camel auction where he will help us select just the beast we need. We try to shake them off, but it's useless. Somewhat rattled, we retreat back inside the lobby where hotel doormen prevent them from following. Bob suggests we try the rear of the hotel, and we race around to the back only to find several of them have anticipated

our move and are waiting for us. We give up at this point and fall back inside for the rest of the afternoon, prisoners of the street "terrorists" outside.

As night falls the entire group of racers assembles to board a large bus which Lamy has indicated will be for a surprise dinner. It's on our printed daily schedule. Bob and I run into Bernard in the lobby and he acts his usual cordial self with us. Evidently, the blowup in St. John's is forgotten. It was a burst of operatic anger that has passed as quickly as it came on. God bless the French.

Our group is bused into the Moroccan night. We leave the city behind and enter the desert. After forty minutes we arrive at a huge lighted structure standing alone on the sands. It's a fort with high turreted walls. Scores of other charter buses are parked by the entrance. Two lines of turbaned and mounted horsemen and camel riders line our way to the front gate. They ululate the wavering falsetto of Arabs and fire their muskets in the air. I'm walking next to Herb Halperin.

*Race director Bernard Lamy with Bob Reiss.*

*Willie Tashima with the Author in Morocco.*

"Christ, Herb. It's Fort Zinderif! I'll bet Brian Donlevy himself is inside, appearing as Sergeant Markov in 'Beau Geste.'"

The place is called Ali's Restaurant and inside the huge fake fort are multiple dining alcoves all around a large open air sand arena. Groups of dancers and musicians representing every ethnic group of Morocco line the walkways as we proceed to our assigned eating area. The noise is deafening. There must be a thousand people employed here.

*The Author spends a quiet evening in Marrakech.*

They come in every conceivable skin color and native costume.

Our group is seated on low cushions, eight to a table. Food is brought. The main course is a whole roast lamb on a large platter for each table. We tear off chunks with our fingers and scarf it down. Delicious! And guaranteed to correct any cholesterol deficiency you may be experiencing. In the middle of all this I feel someone put their hand on my right shoulder. Looking around I find myself staring into the yellow eyes of a striped housecat. He has made his way over on some cushions that line the wall and is now working me for some dinner by putting his front paws on my shoulder and staring hungrily at the lamb. I give him a big piece and he jumps down to the floor to enjoy it. Our group is continuously entertained by wandering bands of dancers and musicians.

After dinner the big show begins. The arena is lit up as a horse drawn wagon comes center. Out pops a scantily attired but muscular lady who does a belly dance for half an hour. She is followed by a wild east show involving horses, camels, mock cavalry charges, and lots of musket fire. A gigantic fireworks display caps the evening's entertainment. Wow!

WEDNESDAY, 4 MAY. After breakfast we attend one of Bernard's press conferences and then a session with representatives of the Moroccan Air Force — they evidently control their country's airspace — who brief us on local air traffic procedures. The weather forecast for tomorrow's flight to Istanbul, Turkey looks good all the way. They request we prepare and turn in our flight plans today.

Istanbul is close to 1,900 nautical miles from here, which is at the very outside edge of our range. The winds will not be much help. Bob approves my plan to make one fuel stop along the way. I have prepared routings for three different stops: Palermo, Sicily; Kerkira, Greece; or Valleta, Malta. Bob observes that he has always wanted to visit Malta, so

*The press conference at Marrakech.*

Malta it is. Besides, everyone speaks English there.

We pass up a guided tour of the souk (native market) and instead take a taxi to the airport where we spend the afternoon fueling and cleaning up the aircraft. Ken Johnson and Larry Cioppi are there too, working on their damaged electronic gear. Ken is some kind of a genius. He actually fixes the black boxes himself and gets everything working again.

This afternoon we hear that two of the race entrants have dropped out and gone home — the Mooney M20 Baccarat from France, and the Merlin LA-Z-BOY from the States. No one seems sure what the circumstances are or why they decided to withdraw. There are rumors that they were unhappy with their own performance, but we never really find out. Bernard Lamy does not make any announcements concerning them and they are soon forgotten. We never really got to know them.

In the evening we have a group dinner at the hotel. The Moroccan dishes are excellent and Bernard is generous with the local wines. Entertainment is provided by several belly dancers who weave from table to table collecting money which is tucked into their costumes as they wiggle vigorously. This is as near as our group is going to get to the fabled fleshpots of North Africa.

## FLASHBACK IV

### "NIGHT MOVES"

VANCE AFB, OKLAHOMA, FEBRUARY 1955.
Our hero, an Aviation Cadet, was in his barracks cot studying for a meteorology test. At 10:45 p.m. his roommate, Stegman, returned from a night VFR student flight in one of the B-25 "Mitchell" bombers then being used in multi-engine training school. Stegman was very pale and his hands were shaking as he put away his headset and oxygen mask.

"What the hell happened to you?"

Haltingly, Stegman related the night's events. He and Cadet Swanson had been tooling around in dark skies at 8,000 feet. Swanson was in the left seat, Stegman was copilot. After an hour or so they decided to switch seats so Stegman could get some pilot time. Now the proper way to do this is for the pilot to unbuckle and stand behind the right seat while the copilot quickly shifts to the left seat. The aircraft, if trimmed, will hold its course for the few seconds this takes.

On this night however, the two took it into their heads to switch seats *simultaneously* by straddling the radio console between the seats with Swanson staying low and Stegman going over the top. They were both small guys and it seemed like a good idea at the time. In the middle of this maneuver two critical events happened: (1) Stegman's backpack parachute snagged against the red handle that trips open the emergency escape hatch in the top of the cockpit and the hatch blew off, and (2) as it did it pulled out the locking pin of Stegman's parachute which popped open and began to feed out the open hatch in the suction of the slipstream. Both Cadets realized they were dead men if any lip of the parachute canopy cleared the hatch and caught in the slipstream. Both of them frantically began to pull at the folds of nylon to keep this from happening. The B-25 flew itself while the two struggled and finally got the parachute inside where it filled the entire cabin in a tangle of nylon and cords. Stegman was eventually able to remove his harness and cram the parachute back out of the way. They came in and landed immediately.

Stegman now had the problem of explaining to the Operations officer: (1) why he opened a parachute inside an airplane, and (2) why the emergency hatch on a particular B-25 was missing.

No formal disciplinary action was taken against either of them, but a month later Stegman got a letter from Base Supply stating he owed the United States Air Force $450 for the missing hatch (Cadets made $100 a month).

# CHAPTER 5

# MARRAKECH TO ISTANBUL

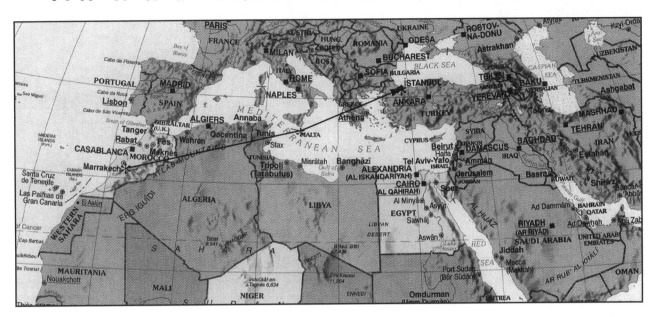

THURSDAY, 5 MAY. We get out to the Marrakech Airport early. There is a full day of flying for everyone and an early start will let us do as much in daylight as possible. 75R is to be among the last group to be released and our scheduled departure time is 0855. It has been our experience that air traffic controllers outside North America are not used to small general aviation aircraft, don't know much about their performance, and generally insist on at least ten minutes spacing between departures.

Things go wrong immediately. It seems Thursday is tourist turnaround day in Marrakech and the airport is busy with incoming and departing airliners full of visitors. Casablanca Control is reluctant to let our group depart as long as they have incoming commercial traffic. This is all bullshit, of course. The weather is clear and any of us would gladly accept a restriction to "climb VFR" to our assigned altitude. Not only will they not give us permission to start engines, they add insult to injury by requiring us to hand push our aircraft back farther to

a corner of the ramp to make room for passenger jet parking. This happens several times. Everyone is frustrated and fuming.

Finally, several of the piston aircraft are given the okay to start engines, but then more delays are imposed. Those that are permitted to taxi out are directed to an area on the other side of the runway and then ignored. They sit there, engines running, while jet airliner after airliner is cleared for landing or takeoff. This spot is soon named "The Penalty Box" among the racers. At last, at long intervals, the racers begin to depart.

At 1015 we are finally allowed to fire up and taxi out. The tower holds us on the taxiway near the approach end of the runway. We sit there, burning fuel uselessly, and wait some more. The wind is shifting from northwest to southwest and now runway 34 is subjected to an 8-10 knot tailwind. I look to my right and see an Air Afrique Boeing 767 turning on a short final. He's too high! I watch in astonishment as the pilot actually *slips* the aircraft with

*The racers on the ramp at Marrakech Airport.*

crossed controls to lose altitude.

"Holy shit, Bob. Look at that!"

I've never seen a large transport slipped before. Just then, there is a burst of excited French on the radio and the 767 brings up both engines for a go-around. With his high approach coupled with the tailwind he has realized he would be too long and has decided to try it again. Everything is confusion on the frequency in both French and English as some incoming pilots want to change to runway 16 and other's don't. It seems that Moroccan air traffic control can get very exciting.

At last there is a gap in the traffic and we are cleared to take the active runway — runway 34. The tailwind is close to 10 knots right now but if we elect to taxi to the other end it would take another fifteen minutes and who knows what other delays? Our gross weight is close to 5,000 pounds and we will have to get nearly 94 knots runway speed to get sufficient flow over the wings for a safe takeoff.

"November 9675 Romeo. Cleared to ERLAM intersection. Maintain flight level one one zero. Contact Casablanca Control on 124.5 before reaching ERLAM."

Happy to have any kind of a clearance, we roll at 1045 (local and Zulu). It's a huge runway so there's no worry about not having enough. After a long run we are airborne and Bob makes a gentle turn to 055

degrees toward ERLAM which is only 118 miles to the northeast. My flight plan was filed for airway R72 to Casablanca (CBA) then airway R975 to Fez (FES), but the ATC clearance, such as it is, sets us directly for Fez but shortstopped at ERLAM intersection about halfway there. We reach 11,000 feet and Bob starts calling Casablanca. No answer is received. We can hear them on the frequency, busy with other traffic, but they do not answer. We're getting close to ERLAM, our clearance limit. As an old Center controller myself, I know very well that, by the rules, we should enter a holding pattern at ERLAM if we don't receive further clearance before we get there. Bob tries Casablanca a few more times but they seem to ignore us. There are no clouds in the sky but a dusty haze limits visibility to about ten miles horizontally. We can see straight down perfectly. Bob gives up on Casablanca Control.

"They won't talk to us. Screw'em. We'll just go on."

"I don't know, Bob. We haven't been cleared anywhere, let alone to Malta. The rules say we're supposed to hold here."

"The rules don't seem to be working today," he replies. "We could wind up holding here all day. We're going on."

ERLAM is crossed, Fez is next, and away we go. At Fez Bob broadcasts our time over and altitude, and my estimate for Oujda on the Morocco/Algeria border. Again, we get no response. Through the haze we begin to make out the shoreline to our left and the Mediterranean Sea beyond. Our flight path will follow the North African coast to Tunis where we will then leave it and fly 198 miles over water to the islands of Malta.

The land below is dry and hard. I've read somewhere that in ancient times North Africa was all forest along the coast but that over the centuries people have cut down the trees to make charcoal. As we fly along over the shore the villages appear to be mostly built on the hilltops while the lowlands are under cultivation. The land is tan in color, the houses are white. It must be difficult to scratch out a living as a farmer down there. Here we are, well fed and bathed and shaved, in an expensive airplane, looking down from above at a way of life neither of us fully understands, nor, God forbid, will ever experience first hand.

Bob is in his historical element. One of his lifelong pursuits is the study of Roman history and he's talking about Scipio Africanus and his defeat of Hannibal, and how the Romans built roads the length of this coast. We pass Oran, Mostaganem and Algiers. Algiers Control answers our radio calls, rogers our position reports, and acts just like everything is normal. My fears about getting into trouble by going past ERLAM intersection without clearance turn into little dots and disperse. Evidently what goes on in Moroccan airspace is of little interest to the Algerians. We are nearing Tunisian airspace now. We dial them up and give Tunis control an estimate for the boundary. Tunisia is only about a hundred miles wide at this point and in forty minutes we are over the capital city of Tunis. It's immense. Well over half a million people live down there in this city built on the ruins of ancient Carthage. It seems that every single building is plastered a dazzling whiteness that makes the whole panorama a sight to behold. We cross the headland that forms the northeast corner of Tunisia and head out over the Mediterranean, bound for Malta.

As soon as we leave the coastline the dust and haze of Africa begin to lighten and in fifty miles we are in an almost clear atmosphere. I try to make out Sicily, which is about ninety miles to our left, but can't see it. The GPS receiver is set on Valletta Airport (LMMI), 130 miles ahead. The Mediterranean is light blue and calm, just as it's supposed to be.

The nation of Malta is made up of three islands — Gozo, to the northwest; the small Comino; and the main island of Malta. The three together are about 32 miles in length. For over 2,000 years they have been owned or occupied at one time or another by every major Eurasian power since they are at the strategic crossroads of the Mediterranean. They were the scene of some of the most intense and prolonged air combat of World War II as the Germans and Italians tried to dislodge the British.

It is near 7:00 p.m. local time when they come into our view (Malta is two time zones ahead of Morocco). The sun is low and its light has taken on a golden flush. The islands are absolutely striking as they stand alone projecting out of the sea. Malta has almost no beaches. Brown vertical cliffs, at least thirty feet high, rise out of the surf up to the main surface of the island where houses and other buildings occupy much of the available space. The long shadows of late afternoon make for dramatic contrasts on this land of the Knights Templar and conquering Eastern armies. Bob and I are fascinated by the beauty, isolation and serenity of this small world below. Here, right here, is the advantage of traveling in a small aircraft. As we let down in preparation for the approach we have a view one could never get from the deck of a cruise ship or the cabin of an airliner. We are paralleling the south coast of Malta at 3,000 feet and the entire island is at our feet. The tan and white buildings of the city of Valletta and the surrounding towns can be seen in sharp detail in the clear air. This is surely one of the major highlights of this trip.

There is no other traffic and we are cleared for approach and landing. Touchdown is at 7:40 p.m. (1740 Zulu) as the sun touches the horizon. Six hours, fifty-five minutes en route. 1,187 nautical miles at 172 knots average ground speed. The tower directs us to the general aviation parking area off on a far corner of the airport away from the passenger terminal. The buildings near our parking area look like leftovers from the war. We confer and it is agreed that Bob will stay with the aircraft and see to the fueling while I take care of whatever paperwork is involved in this interim stop. A friendly citizen on the ramp informs me that while Operations and Meteorology are just inside, Customs and Immigration are, alas, in the main passenger terminal at the other end of the airport; and no, there is no available transport to get me there. I get the impression that Malta does not have a lot of transient general aviation traffic.

I flag down a passing maintenance truck and the driver cheerily agrees to give me a lift. Once at the main terminal I am directed to Immigration where I present both our passports. No problems. Customs, however, is not on duty since no airliners are due for several hours. I must go to their administrative offices in another part of the terminal to file our general declaration forms. An airport official is detailed to guide me there. She is young, redheaded and gorgeous in her trim official uniform. Half in love, I follow her through the large main terminal, up some stairs, and down several corridors to the Customs office. Seven copies of the general declaration are required but they have no copying machine. Several off-duty officers drinking tea pitch in and help me fill out the forms. "Where will you be staying in town sir? You're not staying? You're going straight on? Well, you'll have to fill out seven more copies of an exit declaration for our files."

When this is finally accomplished I am directed back to Immigration in the main terminal for further processing to exit Malta. Passports are examined again, exit cards are filled out, and all the official wickets are hit. Everyone has been courteous and friendly, but by the time I extricate myself and get back to the aircraft I have been away for an hour and a half. Hustling now, I file a flight plan to Istanbul while Bob gets a weather briefing. We saddle up and break ground at 9:46 p.m. (1946 Zulu) bound for Istanbul, 800 miles to the east.

It's another pitch black but clear night as we climb out, leaving the lights of Valletta behind. Our assigned altitude is flight level 110, or 11,000 feet at standard pressure. The clearance we have received is Malta direct BAMBI intersection (cute name!) direct LATAN intersection, then airway G-12 to Istanbul, Turkey. BAMBI intersection is an arbitrary point in the Ionian Sea between Italy and Greece located at North 38.37.7 and East 019.00 on my chart. [Let's see, the .7 at the end of the north coordinate represents seconds of latitude. But there are only 60 seconds to a minute of latitude, so it can't represent 70 seconds. It must stand for .7 times 60, or 42 seconds. More importantly, why am I con-

cerned? Three-tenths of one minute of latitude is only three-tenths of a mile and we will be doing about three miles a minute when we get there. So why am I worrying about a matter of six seconds on the clock? I set the GPS for North 38.38 and East 019.00 and the course for BAMBI appears on the screen.] BAMBI is 274 miles to the northeast of Malta. We are still climbing when suddenly the GPS screen is blinking at me. An "M" is showing in the upper right hand corner of the screen meaning it has a message. I press the "message" button and the words "LOW BATTERIES" appear. What's this? It's not running on batteries but is hard wired into the aircraft's electrical system.

"Something's screwed up with the GPS, Bob. I'm going to shut it down for a while and let it rest. I'll try it again in ten minutes."

"Are we on course for BAMBI?"

"More or less. The winds are forecast as light and variable for this part of the flight. We'll just hold this course. Our estimate for BAMBI is 2121 and if the GPS is still out we'll just report BAMBI at that time."

We level at 11,000 feet and in a while I turn the GPS back on. It goes through its cycle of self checks then begins the process of acquiring satellites. Within two minutes it informs me it is "READY FOR NAVIGATION." I re-program in the BAMBI intersection coordinates and all is as before. Whatever was wrong with it seems to have healed up.

Our original requested routing was BAMBI direct Kerkira VOR in Greece. Our clearance was BAMBI direct LATAN then airway G-12 Kerkira. LATAN intersection lies 45 miles north of BAMBI and marks the line between Brindisi and Athens Flight Information Regions. To go that way will cost us an extra 25 miles — no big deal normally — but we can see no reason for the re-routing except to satisfy some air traffic controller's sense of neatness. It's after eleven at night and we hear no other traffic around. Bob gets on the radio to Rome Control and requests clearance from BAMBI direct Kerkira. Rome says they will have to coordinate with Brindisi and Athens. After fifteen minutes they come back and inform us that Athens will not approve the reroute and leaves us with the unspoken impression that 9675 Romeo should quit bitching and just fly its approved route. Okay, okay.

We hit my estimates for BAMBI and LATAN on the nose and turn eastward toward Greece. Kerkira is on the Island of Corfu, just off the Greek and Albanian mainlands. Damn those Moroccan controllers anyway! If we had been allowed to depart Marrakech at a sensible hour — say like sunup — we would still be in daylight. While planning this trip back at home I always imagined flying over the Greek islands in clear sunshine, and being thrilled to see this ancient cradle of Western thought and civilization for the first time in my life. But here we are, staring down at some scattered lights instead. We might as well be flying over California or the Gulf Coast.

After Kerkira, airway G-12 crosses the mainland of Greece to Thessaloniki then across the north end of the Aegean Sea. (Hey! We're only about fifty miles south of Bulgaria.) Alexandroupolis is our last checkpoint in Greece and we are handed off to Istanbul Control at GOLDO intersection. (That big black area to the right has to be the Sea of Marmara.) The city of Istanbul begins to glow on the horizon. This is no Marrakech. It's brightly lit although it's long after midnight here. As we come nearer, air traffic control descends us to 5,000 feet. Now the city stretches from horizon to horizon, a sea of lights. Our destination is Ataturk International, located somewhere near the center of all this, the main commercial airport serving the city. But there are two other civilian airports and a Turkish Air Force base located here too. Wouldn't it be embarrassing to get them mixed up? Bob has set the frequency of the Ataturk Instrument Landing System on our receiver, but before we have to figure all this out, Istanbul Approach, in a helpful frame of mind, asks us if we would like a radar steer onto the ILS centerline for Ataturk. We would — yes indeed.

There's one other aircraft on the frequency this night. It is not one or our racers, but a commercial jet freighter inbound for Ataturk like us. He's even more dazzled by the lights than we are and requests the same service of a radar steer onto the approach after us.

It is not until we are established on the approach path and gear down, that I finally make out a dark hole in the city with threshold lights at the near end and two strings of runway lights extending away from them. Bob makes his usual smooth touchdown on the huge runway. Our arrival has been at 3:06

a.m. local time (0006 Zulu), four hours and twenty minutes from Malta. We have flown just short of 2,000 nautical miles since Marrakech, through thirty-eight degrees of longitude, and from the Western to the Eastern hemisphere. As we turn off the runway and taxi to the usual far corner of the airport, I realize how tired I am and how good a bed will feel for what remains of the night.

We secure the airplane, are transported to the main terminal, and go through Turkish Customs and Immigration. Our passport numbers and particulars are entered into a computer as we pass through. One of Bernard's minions is there to meet us at this ridiculous hour and he hands me a thick white envelope which, he explains, contains taxi fare plus tip for Bob and me to the Merit Antique Hotel. The envelope is over half an inch thick.

"It feels heavy. How much is in here anyway?"

A shrug. "Oh, about half a million lira."

The taxi takes about twenty minutes. I assume that half a million lira doesn't go nearly as far as it used to.

The Merit Antique is right downtown in the old section of the city and, as we are coming to expect from Arc en Ciel, a splendid establishment. We are very hungry. It has been eighteen hours since we last ate and to our delight the hotel has set aside a private alcove off the main dining room with a table of cold dishes, cheese and wine. Several other race crews are there, late arrivals like us, including Dawn and Gordon Bartsch. We sit around, tiredly, and relate our day's flying adventures to each other. People often think that world flights are conducted in a kind of loose formation, all the aircraft flying together and talking to each other as they go along. That is not so. It is rare for the participants to even see each other while in the air. They are usually so strung out for air traffic separation purposes that they have little idea of what's happening to anyone else on any particular day, so it's good to find out what others have experienced.

Daylight is breaking in Istanbul as we crash into bed.

FRIDAY, 6 MAY. We oversleep a scheduled group boat ride to the Bosphorus so Bob and I have lunch at the hotel. I was having coffee in the lobby when Bernard Lamy came by and we had our first one-on-one chat. Bernard mentions he is a former

*Part of the cityscape of Istanbul.*

disregard for the basic rules of air safety that our Air Force sent all of them packing for home. They would buzz farms and towns, break into landing patterns out of turn, begin acrobatic maneuvers without looking around for other aircraft, and generally ignore all warnings from the American instructors that they were down to their last chance if they kept up this reckless behavior. Bernard and I have a minor male bonding experience as we recall those far-off days on the dusty plains of Texas.

French Air Force fighter pilot. We are about the same age, so I ask him about his early military training. It turns out that he and I went to the same Primary Flying School, Hondo Air Base in Texas! Bernard was an MDAP (Mutual Defense Assistance Pact) student. In the 1950s the United States offered pilot training to foreign officers and cadets from various nations with which we had defense treaties. In my primary pilot class I trained alongside Belgians, Chileans, Cubans and Frenchmen. Bernard had graduated from Hondo just before I arrived so we never met each other. He must have been smarter or luckier than other Frenchmen to have survived the experience. My class had four Frenchmen and all of them were washed out, not for lack of flying ability, but for lack of discipline in the air. They all flew with such elan and

In the afternoon about ten of us take a trip to Istanbul's Old Bazaar. It's a fabulous place but I'm

*A section of the Old Bazaar in Istanbul.*

not much of a shopper. Among the stalls I notice there are a number of currency exchange establishments. Here, I think, is a good chance to get rid of about $30 worth of Moroccan dirhams I have been packing around since Marrakech. I visit several currency shops and am practically laughed out of each place. "Hey, look Achmed! This crazy American is under the delusion that those dirhams are real money. Boy, what a sucker!"

A special meeting of all racers is called for 5:00 p.m. at the hotel to discuss routing for tomorrow's flight to Dubai in the United Arab Emirates. Most of us have planned to fly south to Egypt, cross the Red Sea, and then transit Saudi Arabia to the Emirates which lie at the south end of the Persian Gulf. Others are intending to go the more direct but trickier way of flying through Syria and Jordan before entering Saudi airspace. The most direct route of all would be to go through Iraq, but that is an impossibility because of the United Nations imposed "No Fly" zones there, a leftover from the recent unpleasantness called the Gulf War. This leg of the race, Istanbul — Dubai, has always been the most problematic because of politics, Moslem paranoia, and the general explosiveness of the whole region. Now Bernard drops a bombshell on our group. Although much pre-coordination has been done by Arc en Ciel, the Saudi Arabia Government has pulled the rug from under all our plans by withholding their permission to use their airspace. This has been done at the last minute, and they have offered no reason for it.

All the carefully made plans are now so much trash paper. The only possible way to avoid Saudi airspace is to fly through Iran, to the east of Iraq. We will have to head east from Istanbul to the Turkish-Iranian border and then proceed south through the entire north-south axis of Iran exiting at the Persian Gulf. That's going to be some trip! Can we make it nonstop? We're told it is possible to land in Iran at places like Shiraz and fuel up without prior permission, but does Bernard know this for sure? Do Bob Reiss, former Army intelligence agent, and Dennis Stewart, member of the U.S. Air Force Retired Reserve and former Navy Department official, really want to place themselves at the disposal of the Iranian authorities? Let's look at making it nonstop once more.

I measure the airway mileage from the Jepp charts. By going through Iran it will be 1,709 nautical miles from Istanbul to Dubai International Airport. At 170 knots that will take ten hours. Two hundred and sixty-four gallons of fuel, our maximum load, will give us close to twelve hours endurance. That should be enough even if the winds are adverse. Yes, we'll try it. Flight plans are filled out and given to Bernard for tomorrow's trip.

[Istanbul is one place I am loathe to leave. We haven't seen much of it and there's so much to see. As Byzantium, Constantinople, and now Istanbul, it is one of the oldest cities on earth. It's still vibrant and alive — it's also beautiful. I make a vow to return some day and spend a lot of time here.]

## FLASHBACK V

## "HOME ON THE RANGE"

MARCH 1955. At 2340 hours a B-25 "Mitchell" on a student VFR cross-country training flight was inbound for Vance AFB and journey's end. Fifty miles out the two Aviation Cadets in the cockpit (our hero was in the left seat) tuned in the tower to monitor the local situation.

"This is Vance AFB tower to all area traffic. Local winds, 280 degrees, 10 to 25 miles an hour, are creating an area dust storm. Visibility is now two miles and expected to deteriorate rapidly. All Air Force student traffic should land immediately. Contact Vance tower prior to entering downwind leg."

"Damn," said the copilot. "Sounds like we better get down right away. If we don't we'll have to go to our alternate and we'll miss that engineering final test tomorrow morning."

"Right. I'll start letting down now."

As they descended they sank into the roiling clouds of red dust so common in north central Oklahoma.

"Man, I can't see anything in this crap. Can't find the pattern this way. We're going to have to shoot an instrument approach. I'll keep it high so when we find the field you call us as entering downwind and we'll just do a one-eighty and drop into the pattern."

This plan was in violation of regulations which specified that student pilots were forbidden to make instrument approaches in actual weather conditions without an instructor aboard. Our two heroes were, in effect, attempting to pull a fast one.

The only instrument approach available to Vance AFB in 1955 was an ADF (Automatic Direction Finder) approach off the local Enid commercial radio station, KEND, situated about three miles north of the field. They specialized in country music and as they tuned it in they heard Ernest Tubbs wailing:      "There stands the glass
        Fill it up to the brim
        Til my troubles grow dim.
        It's my first one today."

The ADF needle swung from 0 to 180 degrees indicating they were over the station northbound. The normal course was to fly two minutes north, do a procedure turn, return descending back to the station, then fly a predetermined heading to the field. The next announcement from the station changed all that.

"Well friends and neighbors, I see by the old clock on the wall that it's midnight and the end of another broadcast day. This is KEND, Enid, Oklahoma signing off. G'night everybody." "The Star Spangled Banner" began to play.

Now our national anthem takes only about 65 seconds. *The Guinness Book of Records* does not have a listing for the world's fastest instrument approaches, but that night the "Mitchell" made perhaps the fastest approach ever flown into Vance AFB. The outbound leg was cut to fifteen seconds, the procedure turn was at a sixty degree bank with the throttles closed and the landing gear coming down. They made it back over the station just as the carrier wave shut down, located the field and dropped into the pattern.

As they taxied to the ramp the copilot remarked, "I'll say one thing about flying with you. It's never dull."

# CHAPTER 6

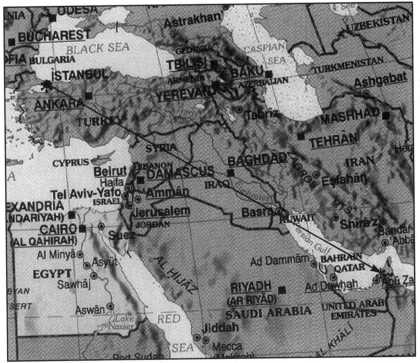

# ISTANBUL

# TO

# DUBAI

SATURDAY, 7 MAY. We are bused to Ataturk International were we must go through Customs and Immigration lugging our own baggage among the regular commercial passengers. Somehow, Carol Lindstrom took a fall out of her airplane onto the ramp when she and her husband arrived. She received medical treatment and is now hobbling around on crutches with a cumbersome brace on her knee. We all hope she heals up quickly.

After the airport processing and another bus ride we reach the race aircraft. Now we must fuel the planes. The airport authorities have made only two fuel trucks available: one jet fuel truck and one gasoline truck. Filling each aircraft separately and then collecting the money is taking forever. We got up this morning at 4:15 in hopes of getting an early start and as much daylight as possible, but our hopes for a quick getaway are being undone. As one of the last planes to arrive we are at the end of the fueling line. I talk to Bernard and make a case that we are by far the slowest of the prop-jets and therefore

should be fueled and released first, but he says there is nothing he can do.

Finally, the fuel truck gets to us. Bob has the aircraft topped off all around: 74 gallons in the mains, 90 gallons in the auxiliary cabin tank and 50 gallons in each tip-tank — 264 gallons in all. 9675 Romeo sags on her landing gear struts and settles with the tail lower than usual. When the tip-tanks are filled their center of gravity is aft of the airplane's center of gravity. Bob gets into the cockpit. When I put my heft on the boarding step in back of the wing the whole plane tips backward and she goes down on her tail — bang — leaving the Bonanza with her nose-wheel in the air and looking silly. I step off, go to the tail and lift it back up. No damage has been done. A Turkish ramp boy is commandeered to hold the tail up while I board the airplane. Bob starts the engine.

Bernard has his usual carefully sequenced departure plan but the chaos of the fueling has screwed everything up. It's every plane for itself now. We taxi out under the cloudy skies and receive our clearance.

"November 9675 Romeo, cleared to Dubai International Airport via direct Yalova Victor Golf eight Elazia Victor eighty-one flight plan route. Maintain flight level one three zero. Contact Departure Control on one two two point seven after takeoff. Squawk one one two six."

Well at least we have a proper clearance this time. We take off at 9:39 a.m. with Bob babying the aircraft through the long roll and climbout. One hundred miles from Istanbul the high overcast begins to break and sunshine lights our world. We are heading almost due east from Istanbul and soon we are over hilly terrain. The Black Sea on our left fades from view. After we pass Ankara the ground below becomes mountainous, the peaks still covered in snow. I see no highways or railroads, no towns or villages down there, just dense forest and mountain tops. Want to get away from it all? Come to eastern Turkey.

We're on VOR/DME airways, each station about 150 miles apart — Gemerek, Elazig, Van — strange sounding names. There is no radar flight following so each checkpoint must be reported and an estimate given for the next. At Van we are four hours and fifteen minutes into the flight. Our next estimate is for BONAM intersection which marks the boundary between Ankara and Tehran FIRs. With visions of blindfolded hostages during 1980 in our heads we call up Tehran Control with our estimate. They answer us matter of factly with the admonition to "maintain one three thousand." We are passing through a narrow corridor of airspace. One hundred miles to the north lie Armenia and Azerbaijan; fifty miles to the south is the border of the dreaded Iraq. There's a big lake below. What is it? I don't know because I never thought to buy ONC terrain charts for Iran and the Jeppesen charts we are using for navigation don't show many ground features. (I found out later it was Lake Urmia.)

We pass south of Tabriz and head for Zanjan. The earth below is no longer forested, but it sure is mountainous — dry brown sharp mountains. Zanjan passes below. We turn southward on airway R54

*Passing over a military base at Esfahan, Iran.*

heading for Saveh, a low-frequency non-directional beacon 125 miles away. Off to our left, beyond the city of Rasht, we can barely make out a broad expanse of blue. It's the Caspian Sea.

By the time we get to Esfahan the sun is getting low. The part of Iran we have crossed so far is very rugged and arid — craggy hills and mountains, all a uniform tan color, with occasional areas of dry looking farms in the valleys. This is a harsh land that must breed tough people. At Esfahan we cross right over a large military air base. The Jepp chart shows it is Badr Air Base, elevation 5,242 feet. Now our course is 165 degrees as we pick up airway R59 for Shiraz, 196 miles to the south.

We have not been able to make all our required position reports. Radio coverage is spotty. They must have very few remote transmitter/receiver sites. We have been out of contact for more than two hours on one section of this route. We report over Shiraz at 1516 Zulu, estimating KASOL intersection at 1539. The Iranian controllers we have talked with so far have spoken excellent English, although they tend to yell very loud if you don't understand them the first time. When we finish the report the controller clears us to "maintain eleven thousand, five hundred feet VFR." Bob gives him a "roger" and starts down.

I'm thinking that they are not really practicing positive control here, only a crude form of flight following. The last airway segment we have flown, between Esfahan and Shiraz, shows on the Jepp chart as minimum altitude 15,000 feet with the minimum terrain clearance at 13,100 yet we flew it at the assigned (we assumed) altitude of 13,000 and nobody said anything. It looks to me that aircraft are free to choose their own flight level and simply keep ATC advised now and then. Now the controller has cleared us to maintain 11,500 but the VFR restriction means "provide your own clearance." I look at the Jepp chart again. Airway A-58 south of Shiraz has a minimum altitude of 13,000 feet with a minimum terrain clearance of 12,500 feet. Let's see now. The sun has set and all ahead lies black. We have no terrain charts since we never expected to go this way, so there's no way to see where the tallest mountains are. It's also almost a sure bet that the Iranians don't put flashing red beacons on top of their mountain peaks.

"Bob," I say, explaining all this, "We're below the minimum terrain clearance altitude for this air-way. I think we ought to go back up to 13,000. I don't think ATC will give a damn if we do."

"But minimum terrain clearance altitudes allow for 2,000 feet clearance over obstacles don't they?"

"I know they usually do. But in this case we're going to be betting our lives on it."

Bob agrees with my thinking and we climb back to 13,000 feet, reporting it to no one.

We are cruising along, in complete darkness, when a very bright red light suddenly appears on the Beechcraft's systems panel. "FUEL PUMP" it reads. Bob immediately throws on the standby fuel pump switch. If the primary fuel pump has failed the engine will soon quit from starvation and the standby pump is the only way to prevent that. There's nothing quite like a bright red light on an instrument panel to focus one's attention, especially over mountainous terrain at night. The engine keeps running smoothly. It hasn't missed a beat. I can see Bob is thinking very hard.

"Either the primary pump has failed or it has to be the auxiliary tank causing it. We used most of the aux tank during the first part of the flight then I shut it off. I turned it on again about half an hour ago. I'll bet the tank has run dry and now the tank's pump is putting some air into the system and giving the main pump's sensors some false readings."

Bob switches off the auxiliary tank's electric pump and in a few seconds the red light goes out. He tests it again, turning the aux tank's pump on and waiting. Soon the pump failure light comes on again. Okay, now we know the cause of the trouble, but it's still mystifying. On our trip through Russia and Siberia in '92 we ran the aux tank dry many times and it never did this. Maybe when the tank was installed again for this trip something different was done. When the pump light is off again, Bob very cautiously reaches out and turns off the standby pump. Nothing happens — incident closed — Whew!

We are coming up on PAPAR intersection which is the limit of Iran's airspace and the beginning of the Emirates FIR. We will be crossing 99 miles of the Persian Gulf just west of the Strait of Hormuz to arrive at Dubai on the other side. The Iranian controller tells us to report PAPAR to Dubai Approach Control and gives us the frequency. Bob thanks the Iranians for their services. All through their airspace they have treated us fair and square. We may represent "The Great Satan" to some of them but it hasn't kept them from acting professionally.

As we pass from land to over the Gulf waters we run into a rainstorm and some turbulence. Dubai has just started us down when the GPS begins to blink at me again with the message "LOW BATTERIES" just like it did climbing out of Malta. What is this? It's no emergency; we're picking up Dubai VOR/DME already, but it's bothersome to have an instrument acting unreliably, especially when we're going to count on it on the over-ocean parts of this trip yet to come. We have two more backup GPS receivers stowed in the aircraft but why isn't this one working right? I turn it off, then on again. It goes through its acquisition routine and comes up working normally. Can it be me that's doing something wrong?

Just as in the comic strips, a tiny light bulb appears over my head. I've been in the habit of turning the GPS on at the start of a trip as soon as the engine starts to run. But wait. I remember that Bob, following correct procedure, always lets the engine spool up completely before he throws the aircraft generator switch on-line. That's it! By turning on the GPS before the current reaches it the unit switches itself automatically to its internal battery power. What a dummy! I've had us flying halfway around the world on battery power. When I turn it off, then on, in the cockpit it goes back to external power and everything is just fine. I'll have to be more careful during startups from now on.

We pass through the rain showers and turbulence. The city and Emirate of Dubai are in front of us now. Bright lights are everywhere. The approach controller sounds British. He gives us a couple of steers to enter the VFR right-hand pattern for Dubai International, another of those airports with huge jetliner sized runways. Bob touches down at 8:59 p.m. local time. We have made it nonstop from Istanbul in ten hours, twenty minutes against sporadic adverse winds — a new all-time endurance record for 9675 Romeo.

We roll along the immense runway in the dark. The tower, now with a different controller speaking with a distinct Scottish burr, tells us to exit the runway to the left at the next taxiway. Bob and I are both searching for the taxiway but can't see it. We bump along in the dark, four eyes peering through the windshield. Have we passed it? We stop, hoping for further directions.

"You know, 75 Romeo, we only allow you to *land* on the runway for free. If you want to rent it for the night, that'll be extra."

Great. Just what we need — a smart-ass tower operator — albeit a very funny one.

"Roger that, tower. Now where is the taxiway?"

"About two hundred feet further on."

We find it and tail a "follow me" truck to the parking area. The night is warm as I unwind from the cockpit and stretch my bones. Ten hours is a long time to sit in one seat, unable to stand or move about. After a few hours in the seat my left knee takes to aching. By experimenting I have found that I can straighten the knee out by putting my foot over the top of the left rudder pedal into the open space beyond. A few minutes of this each hour gives me some relief. Otherwise these long flights would be agony.

At the main airport terminal we go through the formalities quickly and are directed to a taxi already pre-engaged to take us to our hotel. Our vehicle is a Mercedes with fancy white seat covers and doilies. The driver is dressed in native clothing with a flowing white robe that reaches to his sandaled feet, and a flowing headdress à la Lawrence of Arabia. He speaks no English. We drive out of the city and into the night desert listening to native music on the car radio whose volume is set about two clicks above the critical decibel level. To my Western ears the atonality of the music, coupled with its deafening volume, is not my idea of a relaxing end to a long day.

The Emirate of Dubai, with all its oil money, has built an excellent network of roads. They stretch out over the sands, flat and smooth, and our driver takes full advantage of them, often topping 144 kilometers per hour (90 mph). After an hour of speeding through the night we begin to see large lighted industrial structures. They look like port installations with huge cranes and warehouses.

Standing alone on the desert shore of the Persian Gulf is the Jebel Ali Hotel, a modern multi-storied resort, one of the Arc en Ciel's corporate sponsors and our destination for this night. It is a playground for rich Arabs and their European guests. The vast lobby is lined with portraits of Emirs of the past. The hotel staff are from all over the world. Filipinos, Japanese, Indonesians, assorted Europeans, Americans, and more. They are there to see that we

they landed at Shiraz, not really knowing what to expect. There they were, three foreign ladies, visa-less and unveiled, one of them in her seventies, dropping in unannounced on a country not only hostile to America, but where the *Koran* is the civil law of the land. What happened? Nothing really. The Iranian airport personnel pumped them some gasoline, collected the U.S. dollars they offered, and wished them well. In and out in thirty minutes. They didn't even have to file a new flight plan.

*Left: The author outside the Jebel Ali Hotel in Dubai.*

*Below: A view of the front of the Jebel Ali Hotel.*

enjoy our stay. After registration we are directed to a section of the dining room where the other race teams are relaxing after the day's flight. A buffet has been prepared for our supper. The food is European, plentiful, and very good.

While swapping stories with the other crews we find out that one team actually stopped in Iran to refuel. It was the all-female crew of Ringenberg, Foggle and Schiff flying the Cessna 340 *Spirit of '76*. Low on fuel,

THE RACE SO FAR. Dubai is roughly the halfway point in the race. In the Turboprop category, Vijaypat Singhania in Tiger is in front with the Lindstroms in their Cessna Conquest Oak Lawn Express a very close second. Both are serious about winning, Hors Ligne is third. The Spirit of San Diego prop-jet Bonanza is a very distant fourth and getting farther behind with every leg.

The turbocharged piston category is turning into a close race between the two Cessna 210's, *Go Johny Go* with Erik Banck and Merce Inglada, and *Norway* with the two Norwegians, Stephansen and Roang. *Kona Wind*, flown by the Bartschs, is third.

The other category, Piston (normally aspirated) is being fought out by *Zephyrus*, the Glasair III, and the Twin Commanche *Tail Wind World Flyer*, with the Glasair slightly in the lead. Willie Tashima and Herb Halperin in the Bonanza are not officially placed at the moment because they were left behind in Istanbul when their radio went out. As soon as they can arrange for repairs, they will catch up with us.

Many miles are yet to be flown.

SUNDAY, 8 MAY. The morning and afternoon are free, with nothing scheduled. Bob and I stroll around the luxurious hotel grounds, the beach and the yacht basin. A group lunch is held, al fresco, on the terrace with hotel staff barbecuing something and great piles of fresh fruit and melons on the tables.

Before dinner Bernard holds a press conference followed by a planning session for tomorrow's flight to Agra, India. It turns out that Agra is in the area where Vijaypat Singhania grew up, so Bernard asks him if there are any local conditions we should be aware of before we get there.

Vijaypat, who has not had a lot to say up to this point, warns us that the airport at Agra regularly experiences reduced visibility in the afternoon because of smoke from cooking fires in the nearby city. In this dry pre-monsoon season we can expect no more than one or two miles visibility during approach.

"..... and then there are the bluebulls."

"Bluebulls?"

"Yes, large wild cattle, sacred to my people, who often wander onto the runways. If you hit one you will be in a great deal of trouble. There are lots of them around Agra."

An excited murmur comes from the group. This has their attention.

"How big are they?" asks one of the Norwegians, alarmed now.

"Very big. As big as one of your elks — what I think the Canadians call a moose. They are not afraid of airplanes and will just walk in front of you when you land."

As Vijaypat says this we begin to see a smile start to play on his lips. We've been had! Indians are not noted for their sense of humor, at least not outside of India, but this one has caught us flatfooted. We all have a laugh at our own expense.

After nightfall a bus is brought around and we are all taken a long distance out into the desert and unloaded by an encampment of Arab tents. Whole sheep are being turned on spits over charcoal. Female fortune tellers have set up shop under a canopy for

*The pool of the Jebel Ali Hotel in the foreground with the Persian Gulf in the background through the trees.*

our amusement, and a saddled camel and its handler are standing by for photographs. All this is just for our group. We are the only ones here. Beer and wine are served. Good food is important to the French, and Bernard is treating us very well.

Jim Knuppe is the captain of *Arc en Ciel II*, a Cessna Citation executive jet. Jim, his copilot Mike Wilson, and Mrs. Knuppe are not racing but have come along, with entrance fee waived, to be our advance plane. They depart long before anyone else, sometimes a full day ahead, checking the weather and trying to make sure that all arrangements at the next airport are in order. Jim is an outspoken and ebullient sort, always cheerful. He is also a fervent born-again Christian. This latter quality, rumor has it, got him in a tangle with Lamy today when Bernard found out he was giving out copies of the New Testament to members of the hotel staff and anyone else who wanted one. That kind of activity may be commendable back home, but in an Islamic country it can be a serious felony. He was told, in no uncertain terms, to knock it off.

Now Jim and his wife are climbing on the camel for a photograph. Mrs. Knuppe is in the saddle while Jim sits on the rump. The camel, muzzled for the occasion, has a wild look in his eyes. When it is time to dismount, the handler gives the beast a light whack on the shin with a stick. The camel lurches suddenly onto his front knees which causes Mrs. Knuppe to be catapulted out of the saddle and onto the camel's neck where she clings tightly. Alarmed by this strange development, the camel stands up again which causes Mrs. Knuppe to lose her grip and drop sharply to the sand. Fortunately, she lands on her back. The camel is now confused and excited. He tries to turn and get away, and in doing so his hooves miss her head by only an inch. The handler gets him under control while others rush in and drag Mrs. Knuppe away. It was a close call. What an irony it would be to fly half way around the world

*Bob Reiss with a chef at the desert feast in Dubai.*

only to be trampled by a camel.

Dinner is served in a large Bedouin tent floored with rugs while we sit around on cushions. I'm glad I like mutton because that's about all we've been served in Dubai. We are entertained by the usual belly dancers.

Our bus returns us to the Jebal Ali Hotel at a reasonable hour. That's good. Tomorrow night we will sleep in Agra, India, thirteen hundred nautical miles to the east.

## FLASHBACK VI

*(Note: After graduation from USAF Pilot Training, our hero was assigned to Pacific Division MATS as a copilot on C-124 Globemaster four-engine transports, the last of the great piston-powered heavy lifters.)*

## "OOOPS!"

It was the mid-1950s. Eisenhower was in the White House, and all was right with the world. On a summer's afternoon a giant C-124 Globemaster four-engine transport, loaded with general cargo, was one hundred and twenty-five miles off the coast from San Francisco inbound to Travis AFB from

Honolulu. It had been a routine flight for the last nine hours. They had penetrated the North American Air Defense Identification Zone on time and in the required sector, and now both pilots were in the cockpit preparing for the descent and landing to come. In the left seat sat a Major, a World War II and Korean War veteran bomber pilot, and a man of vast experience in the air. To his right sat a 2nd Lieutenant (our hero), gung ho and eager to make good, who had passed his checkout as second pilot a scant two months before.

The flight engineer, sitting at his console behind the cockpit, suddenly had his attention focused by an amber light on his trouble board. "Engineer to Pilot. I have a generator overheat warning light on number three."

"Roger, feather number three."

There was little choice. A thermal sensor on the generator had detected an abnormal amount of friction heat, probably from a failing bearing. This could lead to an accessory section fire, a condition to be avoided. The only safe way to restart the engine was to disconnect the offending generator. It could be reached in flight through a crawl tunnel in the wing which led to the accessory section of each engine. Once there, a crew member could take a generator off-line by two different methods: (1) he could put a large screwdriver into a special slot at the base of the generator while the flight engineer slowly unfeathered the engine thereby snapping the generator drive shaft, or (2) remove the entire generator from the engine itself, far more time consuming but enabling the expensive generator to be repaired and salvaged. The second engineer was dispatched to take care of it. Inching worm-like through the narrow tunnel, he reached the number three engine. The floor of the tunnel was a 12" wide metal plank that made a hump over the large double truck right main landing gear in number three nacelle. Perched on this hump, he plugged in his portable intercom and requested permission to remove the generator manually.

"OK, Sarge, but make it snappy. We'll be landing at Travis in about thirty minutes."

Air Traffic Control was advised of their situation and a "Dumbo" SA-16 Albatross was scrambled at Hamilton AFB to accompany them in. Time passed.

A long slow descent was established. Over San Francisco they could see the Travis weather was clear. Tension relaxed on the flight deck, then suddenly increased again.

"Engineer to pilot. Number one prop is surging. Does not respond to control. It's starting to over-speed!"

"Reduce manifold on number one and see if you can keep it under the red line." As the number one throttle came back the gear warning horn sounded loudly in the cockpit and the gear handle lit up with a bright red light.

"Dammit! Let's get this thing on the ground right now. Cancel our IFR and ask Travis for a straight-in approach." The copilot got on the radio and received the clearance. They neared the field.

"All right. Gear down, flaps twenty degrees." The copilot slammed down the gear handle and reached for the flap control as he repeated the command. "Gear coming down, flaps ....."

"AAAAIIIEEEEEEEEEEEEEE!"

"What was that? Oh Sweet Jesus, Sarge is in #3 nacelle!"

"Gear up!" The copilot lifted the handle.

"YEEEEEEEEEOOOOOOOOOOOW!"

"Sarge, you OK?"

"Yessir, but GODDAMN!"

"Forget the generator. Get out of there quick and buckle in. We're landing."

Later, on the taxiway, the Major was very quiet, but the copilot attempted an apology. "Gee, Sarge, we're really sorry. We got all worried about #1 and kind of, heh, heh, forgot about you. No hard feelings?"

The second engineer, now serving as ground scanner with his head and shoulders sticking out of the top of the aircraft, did not reply.

Several days later the Sergeant, feeling better, told the Lieutenant that it was bad enough when the gear doors opened all of a sudden and he got hit with a 160 knot wind while looking down 3,000 feet, but what really scared him was when the gear came back up and stopped just four inches from his face.

# CHAPTER 7

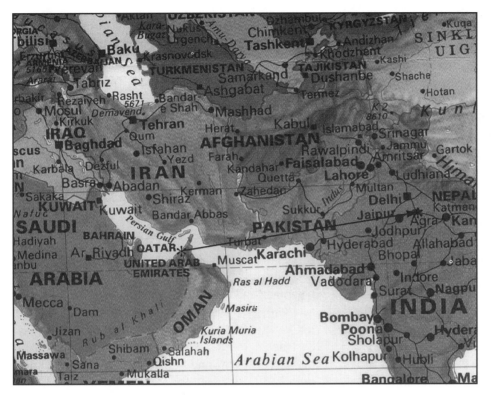

# DUBAI

# TO

# AGRA

MONDAY, 9 MAY. The fueling here at Dubai is fast and efficient if you are taking on jet fuel. The gasoline burners must be fueled from some rusty looking drums on the back of a pickup truck. The weather is clear. We depart at 9:36 a.m. cleared all the way to Agra at 13,000 feet.

Our flight path today will take us through the airspace of five different countries. We are starting in the Emirates Flight Information Region but just fifty-nine miles to the east we will enter the Muscat FIR of Oman as we start to cross the Gulf of Oman just south of the Strait of Hormuz. Only twenty-nine miles later, still over the Gulf, we will be in Iranian airspace and talking to Tehran Control. Staying over the water a few miles south of the coast of Iran we will make landfall at Jiwani, Pakistan, which puts us within the Karachi FIR. At Jiwani we plan to turn northeast picking up airway G214D which will set us on an almost direct course for Delhi, India. Our destination, Agra, lies 110 miles southeast of Delhi. The total mileage is 1,319, almost half of which will

be in Pakistan. We don't know it when we start out, but by the end of the day the air traffic controllers will cause us to fly an extra 75 miles.

The aircraft is not topped off with fuel, nor is the day particularly warm, so our liftoff is relatively easy. We climb out, make radio contact with Muscat Control to let them know we will be entering their airspace, and settle into the flight. With each leg of this journey our confidence in the Bonanza and its fuel system has grown. By now, we are sure that it can, with due care, handle loads far in excess of its normal parameters. Having an extra 120 horsepower in the nose makes a great difference.

The Gulf waters below us are pale blue. They don't look very deep. At IMLOT intersection Bob tries Tehran Control but gets no answer. Over KANAS intersection at 0626Z, a compulsory reporting point, we still are not answered. The southern coast of Iran off to our left is brown and treeless.

The Jepp chart has several boxed warnings stating that one cannot enter Tehran FIR without contacting their Air Defense Radar on 134.10. We've tried that too with no result. Maybe we're too low for good communication. The Bonanza is capable of flying at altitudes of 20,000 feet or even higher, but it's not pressurized and we would have to be wearing oxygen masks. The oxygen supply is limited to four hours or less with two of us breathing from it and we want to save it for situations where we may have no choice but to use it to get over high terrain or bad weather. There's another factor at play here. Both of us see a part of this adventure as the world's greatest sightseeing trip and you can't see much of the earth from high altitudes. Some of the others are missing a lot up there at 27,000 feet going over 300 knots. To our way of thinking, they might as well have bought a commercial jet ticket for the trip.

Seventy miles from Jiwani we contact Karachi Control and give them an estimate for their FIR.

We're over land once more. Pakistan looks almost lunar in its bleakness. The annual monsoons will not be here for another month and the dry season has been long. It is not until June that central Asia really heats up and the rising air from the Gobi Desert creates a low pressure area that draws in the moist winds from the Indian Ocean along with the heavy rains they bring. Most of India, Bangladesh and Southeast Asia are subjected to the heavy rains all through the summer. I'm sure that Bernard chose May to stage this race for that very reason, to avoid the monsoon. Of course the offset of all this has resulted in our flying the North Atlantic three weeks earlier in the year than did Lindbergh, and the fact that we will be traversing parts of Siberia and Alaska at a time of the year when the weather is most fickle.

We pass Panjgur VOR at 0832, altering course slightly to 076 degrees magnetic for SHANO intersection. Karachi, the capital of Pakistan, is 200 miles to the southeast. We won't even come close to it. Forty minutes later we are nearing SHANO when Karachi Control calls us.

"November 9675 Romeo, we have a new clearance for you."

"75 Romeo, go ahead."

"November 9675 Romeo is cleared to Jaipur VOR by SHANO direct NH airway B210 KE airway 462. Maintain flight level one three zero."

Where the hell is Jaipur? (I don't even know how it's spelled.) I'm scanning the chart rapidly.

There's Rahim Yar Khant VOR (RK) ahead and it's the only one between here and Delhi VOR, 360 miles beyond.

"This is 75 Romeo. Please repeat the clearance."

While the controller is repeating, both of us are searching the chart. There's Jodhpur VOR, but that doesn't seem right (Isn't that a kind of riding boot?). Finally, Bob spots Jaipur (JJP) in the upper right hand corner of the map. It's 126 miles south of Agra but equidistant with Delhi from it. I trace the clearance backward from Jaipur and see that they are sending us on a detour far to the south of the large blank part of western India where there seem to be no airways. This is probably at the request of Delhi Control. They want to keep these strange little foreign aircraft away from the commercial jet traffic around the Indira Gandhi International Airport that serves their nation's capital.

Okay, we've finally got it. Bob reads back the clearance and at SHANO we starboard the autopilot to 150 degree magnetic for Nawabshah (NH).

After Char (KE) radio beacon we are headed east again for RAMSA intersection, the boundary between Pakistan and India. The outside air temperature has been rising for the past several hours. As we cross the invisible border it reads 22 degrees Centigrade — that's 72 degrees Fahrenheit at 13,000 feet! We are over the great plains of central India. The ragged hills of Pakistan are behind us and below the featureless earth, bone dry and a uniform tan color, stretches out in all directions. It is far from empty, however. Small villages are everywhere, collections of huts surrounded by barren fields. They dot the landscape as far as we can see. The sky above us is bright pastel blue but below the atmosphere is dense and brown. The dry lands are giving up their topsoil to the winds. The vast clouds of dust rise to 12,000 feet. Neither of us has ever witnessed anything like this before.

We finally arrive at Jaipur VOR. Bob is talking to Agra Approach Control and we are cleared direct to the Agra Airport (VIAG), about one hour ahead. They are reporting one and a half miles visibility in haze and dust. Vijaypat's weather prediction has come true.

The Agra Instrument Landing System is down for maintenance, so Approach Control offers us a precision radar approach to the north-south runway and Bob accepts. This is getting interesting. I haven't been involved in a GCA (Ground Controlled Approach) in over thirty years, since my Air Force days. We've been told that Agra is an Indian Air Force base that is open to joint use, so I'll bet the approach controllers are all military.

The controller steers us onto the centerline for the runway. The phraseology he uses is familiar to my ears.

"Three miles from touchdown. On course, one hundred feet high. Increase rate of descent slightly. That's good — very good ........."

Bob flies the approach like an old pro. At one mile I call the runway in sight and we land at 6:08 p.m. (1338 Zulu. Agra is in one of those odd time zones, like St. John's, that are half an hour out of sync with Universal time). As we taxi in I see further proof that we are in some kind of a time warp. There are Indian Air Force aircraft parked all around. I see C-47's, a Constellation, and half a dozen B-57 Canberra bombers. It's like a trip back to the 1950s.

We park alongside the other race aircraft. The leg has taken eight hours, two minutes, 1,395 nautical air miles (1,602 statute miles) at an average speed of 174 knots. As Bob shuts down the aircraft it is surrounded by smiling people. We get out and are mobbed by well-wishers who shake our hands and place floral wreaths around our necks. There are civilians, women, children, uniformed military, and various government officials, all smiling and welcoming us to India in the last light of the day. Bob helps several children up to sit in the Bonanza's cockpit.

We are directed to Immigration where our visas are inspected and passports scrutinized then stamped. The officials laboriously write down our names, then others check the spelling. Everyone is smiling but this takes half an hour as we stand in the enveloping and enervating heat. Finally through with Immigration, we are led over to Customs which is in an even hotter wooden passenger terminal. Our general declaration — which declares nothing — is read carefully. We are asked to produce any cameras we have. Bob unpacks his Nikon and the serial number is noted down. I rummage into my duffel and dig out the small Kodak "Smilesaver" I've brought along. A Customs official inspects it and smilingly informs me that it is a very cheap camera and beneath their official notice. Thanks. It has taken five officials forty minutes to inspect us. I now

believe everything I have ever heard about the fabled Indian governmental red tape and bureaucracy.

We make our escape from the Customs area and are directed to a waiting car containing a driver and some other functionary in the front seat. We will later become aware that we are now on Vijaypat Singhania's home turf. He is a man of wealth and power, very well connected, and he has seen to it that all the racers and members of Arc en Ciel are to be treated well and are, in effect, his guests while in Agra. As we leave the airport a large banner strung over the road reads "WELCOME TO ALL RACERS. GOOD LUCK VIJAY."

The night ride into town from the airport will stay in my memory forever. The roads are incredibly crowded with every kind of conveyance imaginable — cars, motorcycles, bicycles, pedestrians, oxcarts, rickshaws, pedicabs, camels with huge loads of wood on their backs, motor scooters, trucks, jeeps, buses, pushcarts, and among all this wander the sacred cows (bluebulls?) blinking with bewilderment at the chaos around them. Most of the vehicles have no lights or reflectors showing. Everyone who has a horn is blowing it constantly. The opposite flowing lanes of traffic overlap in the center of the road in a head-on contest of wills to see who can bluff his way through and make the other fellow play chicken. Bob and I sit in the rear seat pop-eyed at this incredible scene as our driver takes nearly impossible risks as he alternately accelerates, brakes, and twists through the crush.

Just as we are turning into the hotel, the inevitable happens. A jeep in front of us slams into a bicycle carrying two teenagers. The boys are thrown violently onto the pavement as the bicycle is crushed beneath the jeep's front wheels. I'm sure they are seriously injured but what can I do? Our driver ignores the incident as if it were an everyday occurrence, which it probably is.

When we get to our room at the Taj View Hotel we find printed invitations on our beds. Mr. Vijaypat Singhania would be honored by our attendance this evening at a reception to be held in the hotel gardens, dress optional.

As we arrive in the gardens the party is in full swing. The hotel grounds are strung with festive lights. Food pavilions are all over the grass. Entertainers sing and dance to a traditional Indian orchestra and several bars are dispensing drinks. At

*A spectacular view of the Taj Mahal and the beautiful grounds leading up it it.*

least a hundred attendees, Europeans and Indians, are there enjoying themselves. Bob and I are ravenous. As usual, we've had nothing since breakfast. Arc en Ciel has faithfully supplied all air crews with box lunches for each day's flight but we are in the habit of refusing ours. Neither of us wants to be bothered by any more clutter in the cockpit than necessary. Besides, a filling noon meal can develop into a sleepy afternoon's flight and we want to stay alert. To avoid dehydration Bob has his thermos of coffee and I suck on some bottled water from time to time. Now, the day's flying over, we head straight for the food. Each pavilion holds one or two dishes, each different from all the others. There is European style cuisine and Indian, too. It's all good.

After dinner we mingle and meet. All educated

*Left:*

*Building on the grounds of the Taj Mahal compound.*

*Below:*

*Bob Reiss at one of the entrances to the Taj Mahal.*

Indians speak fluent English and there is no awkwardness. The Indian women are exotically beautiful in their flowing saris. The males are in uniform or Western business attire. We're still in our flying suits, sweat-stained and probably smelly, but everyone is very gracious to us.

TUESDAY, 10 MAY. After breakfast two buses pick up our entire group and we head for the Taj Mahal. When Bob and I arose this morning the Taj View Hotel lived up to its name. Right in the center of our 4th floor room's picture window the famous tomb stood in the morning light about half a mile away.

On our way there we get a close-up daylight look at the streets of Agra. A travel agent friend once told me that the average American tourist in India has nothing in his or her background to prepare them for the shock of seeing the poverty of India for the first time. The streets are full of idle people. Gaunt men, wearing nothing but loincloths, stand motionless in the shade of trees, most likely focusing on how they can get their next meal. The tiny shops are

*Bob Reiss standing with two soldiers at the Taj Mahal.*
*Two tourists are resting in the background.*

just lean-tos with few goods to sell. Human despair is everywhere. The children break your heart.

At the Taj Mahal we do our tourist duty. It is, as advertised, one of the most beautiful man-made objects in the world. Along the river about a mile away we can see the Red Fort. It is hot and getting hotter. Bob and I spend some time inspecting a lawnmowing rig pulled by two sacred cattle. You can't kill them but that doesn't mean you can't work them.

There are soldiers all over, armed with World War II British Enfield .303 caliber bolt action rifles. Inside the tomb's burial chamber it feels thirty degrees hotter than outside. The bus operator thoughtfully dispenses cold soft drinks as we reboard. From the sublime we move on to the ridiculous, and are bused to a rug merchant's emporium where some locals do their high pressure best to sell us hand-woven rugs. They meet with very little success.

Something quite special is laid on for lunch. The bus takes us to a

*Above:*
*One of the "lawnmowers" utilized*
*for the grounds outside*
*the Taj Mahal.*

*Right:*
*The view from the side*
*of the Taj Mahal.*

*Bob Reiss visiting with the owner and some young boys in one of the factories in Agra.*

Bob was truly affected by the poverty and suffering he saw in Agra and wrote the following:

*Agra, India, home of the Taj Mahal, one of the most beautiful pieces of architecture in the world, speaks of splendor and unfailing love. It is situated, however, within the environs of the most unspeakable crushing poverty one can imagine. For Americans, one must see, smell and taste it, for we are incapable of imagining it.*

*After departing the airport on a tropical evening with not a breath of wind, we view, on the way to the hotel, a horde of humanity on top of one another, and stuffed into every available crevice. Men, women and children by the thousands — skinny, frail, oozing sickness and despair — and the smell, yes, the smell — the smell of*

luxury hotel where the city fathers of Agra are set to host a special welcome for our group. As we enter, each of us gets marked with a red dot in the center of his or her forehead. It looks like every important person in town is there. All of us are arranged on floor cushions with low tables in front of us. The food is Indian and exotic. Some dishes come covered in thin genuine silver foil. (This is the meal I suspect of causing almost half the racers to fall seriously ill within 24 hours.)

After lunch speeches are made, always with a special tribute to Vijaypat, and all race participants are given a silver memorial plate as a souvenir.

*These colorful "pedicabs" were used for touring within parts of Agra. The sign in the background welcomes the world racers.*

*Racer and tycoon Vijaypat Singhania who arranged for a lavish reception and welcome for all the racers in Agra.*

death, feces, urine mixed with hot spices and cow manure burned for fuel. This is the face of poverty — real, true abject poverty. As awful as some circumstances may be in the United States, I vow to never, never again accept the claim that poverty exists in the U.S. Not to this scale, not to this extent of suffering, not to this level of hopelessness. This in front of me is poverty, a sight and smell I will never forget and which racks my soul with anguish and compassion.

In the morning we will see "death carts" — hand-drawn, stacked with those who laid down last night and found, in lying down, their final resting place. Unrelenting this goes on, 365 days a year. The people endure — they can't

*Who is learning about whom in this scene in Agra, India?*

*One of the young boys working in a small factory — a cheerful smile for the camera.*

*An artisan busy at work in Agra.*

*imagine a better life, or at least a way out of their misery, just as we cannot imagine what their short emaciated existence must be like. If you want to wage a war on poverty, go to India. You have a new social theory for human kind? First try it in India. You have a new secret for well-being and happiness? First share it with those most in need — from my per-*

*spective, I have never seen a greater need for it than in India. I asked our Indian hosts "How could this happen?" They shrugged and said, "It just happens."*

In the evening the group is taken to the air base to receive an elaborate weather briefing for tomorrow by the Indian Air Force. They've gone to a lot of trouble and we appreciate it. As for me, I'd rather have a shorter but more accurate weather brief just before departure in the morning when everyone would have a better picture of what the weather actually *is*, not what they think it will be tomorrow.

Afterwards, the air base hosts a grand reception and dinner for us on the lawn outside. The Air Marshall of the Indian Air Force himself has come from New Delhi to preside over the festivities. Food, drink, entertainers, and a large sign "WELCOME AIR RACERS" made of electric bulbs make for a gala affair. In the middle of all this who should walk in but Dr. Willie Tashima and Herb Halperin. They ran into many delays getting their radio repaired in Turkey and by pressing on through Dubai, have just caught up with us. They get a rousing welcome from all.

Our group is overwhelmed by the hospitality shown us by the Indians. They do us no favor, however, by keeping us up past midnight before the buses return us to the hotel. Our breakfast in the morning is scheduled for 0500 and it should prove to be a very long day for all as we attempt to fly to Ho Chi Minh City in Vietnam.

## FLASHBACK VII

### "TO CATCH A THIEF"

NOVEMBER 1955. It had been our hero's first trip to the Philippines. He was a very junior copilot. The C-124 Globemaster had departed Travis AFB three days ago. After twelve hours crew rest in Hawaii they had gone on to Wake Island. From Wake, they had flown on to NAS Agana, Guam, rested again, then flown to Clark AFB in the Philippines. They had crossed numerous time zones and the International Date Line, and by now the Lieutenant had lost all track of time. After landing at Clark at about 2:00 a.m. local time the crew had made straight for the Bachelor Officers' Quarters and some needed rest.

In the un-air conditioned world of the 1950s, the BOQ was a large, high ceilinged, plantation-like structure with wide screened-in porches all around to catch any breeze that might help cool the occupants. Each room had four cots and was connected to the porch by a swinging door reminiscent of old western saloons. Our hero had a room to himself.

Around dawn he was partially awakened by the squeak of a rusty hinge on the swinging door. He cracked an eye and beheld a small Filipino native, shoeless, tip-toeing through the room. The intruder crossed the room to the wardrobe and picked up the Lieutenant's shoes, then turned and began creeping toward the door! The Lieutenant, now fully awake, sprang from his cot with a roar.

"Got ya, you little bastard!" he shouted as he spun the man around and slammed his back against a wall. "Steal my shoes will you?"

The Filipino's eyes were wide with terror. He began screaming in Tagalog. Their combined yelling roused the entire BOQ and a crowd of men in their underwear came running down the porch toward the Lieutenant's room. They were shouting, too.

Just as the pandemonium reached its peak, the BOQ Manager, also in his underwear, arrived on the scene. After quieting the mob down, he explained to the Lieutenant that it was part of the BOQ's service to polish their guests' shoes each night. Since the Lieutenant had neglected to place his shoes outside before retiring, the houseboy, just doing his job, had entered the room to collect them.

Our hero, thoroughly mortified, explained to the assembly that he was ignorant of local customs and sorely regretted the incident. When he checked out that evening, he slipped the houseboy a fat tip.

# CHAPTER 8

# AGRA TO HO CHI MINH CITY (SAIGON)

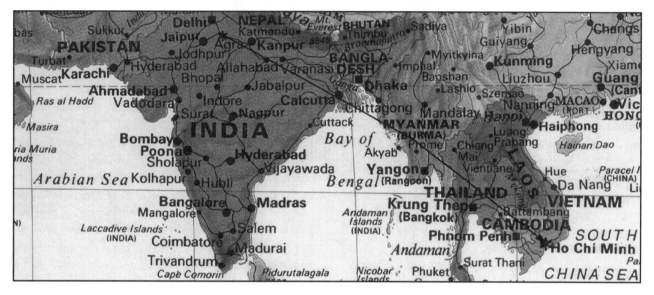

WEDNESDAY, MAY 11. At 6:00 a.m. we leave for the airport. The fueling of the planes goes reasonably well for everyone except us. There seems to be a rule throughout Asia that even the most basic task must be performed by at least a three-person team. No fewer than four employees of Indian Oil are seeing to the fueling of Bob's Bonanza. As they are filling the internal auxiliary tank they get into a lively conversation, in Hindi, which seems to turn into an argument. They are so involved in this debate that they forget to watch the filler neck in the tank and when it is full the high pressure nozzle sloshes jet fuel all over the inside of the cabin. At least a gallon has been spilled on our gear and the mat that lines the floor of the cabin. Bob and I set to work with paper towels to sop up the mess while the truck crew apologizes profusely. It will be several days before the reek of kerosene fades from the aircraft.

Now a final hurdle must be leaped before we can leave. Squads of civil servants recheck our passports, give us forms to fill out, and then write down our names on lists that are compared to the lists on which they wrote our names when we arrived. I've never seen anything like it.

Let's get going! It's 8:15 in the morning and it's hot already. We are determined to attempt this flight to Vietnam nonstop and it is 1,900 nautical miles from here to there. Bob has taken on as much fuel as he dares — main and auxiliary tanks full (164 gallons) and 60 gallons in each tip-tank (total: 284 gallons). That should give us well over twelve hours of endurance. The en route winds are forecast to be from the north or northeast so we will not get any help there.

The Bonanza has never flown this heavy before. The temperature is getting close to 90 degrees and that won't help either. We start up, taxi out, receive our ATC clearance to Saigon, and after some delay, are cleared for takeoff.

[At this point in this narrative it would be best to quote Bob Reiss directly on the technical aspects of handling an overgross takeoff. In the best engineering tradition, Bob has shared this knowledge with others in an article published in the World Beechcraft Society journal, to which he is a contributing editor. It reads, in part, as follows:]

*Because of uncertainties that existed in fuel stops en route from Agra, India to Ho Chi Minh City (Saigon), Vietnam, I decided to fuel the prop-jet Bonanza to the maximum limit that I had previously considered my personal outer edge. That weight on takeoff was 5,400 lbs. The certificated gross weight of the prop-jet A36 Bonanza is 3,860 lbs. The percent over certificated gross weight was 40%. That is 1,540 lbs. over weight.*

*The runway conditions were smooth, near sea level, hot (91° F), and long (12,000 feet). The standard day power for the prop-jet is 420 hp compared to the IO 550 @ 300 hp. Arithmetically, I figured that I could safely lift the load based on the excess HP I had available. I had previously researched record setting Bonanza flights and concluded for myself that at zero excess G loading the airplane would not precipitously fail. I concluded that I **would not** test the envelope, however, and I would not do anything to induce G forces. I had also calculated that the stall speed of the airplane at this weight would increase to 85 kts (I round everything up to be on the safe side). So my plan for takeoff was to not even attempt to let the A/C fly until I had an air speed indication of 85 kts.*

*Yes, I was concerned about the tires and had consulted about what the extra speed might do to the tires and concluded that I would not at this speed precipitate an automatic overheated tire and blowout. (I also put new tires and tubes on before the ATW flight.) I had also convinced myself that the landing gear was safe for up to 7,200 lbs.*

*Now before attempting this takeoff, I had slowly been approaching this gross weight. Starting back in the U.S. I had proceeded as follows:*

| | | |
|---|---|---|
| *1st TO* | *Certificated gross weight* | *+10%* |
| *2nd TO* | *Certificated gross weight* | *+15%* |
| *3rd TO* | | *+20%* |
| *11th TO* | | *+40%* |

*In other words, I slowly approached the 40% OGW limit looking for those slight changes in A/C behavior that I hoped would signal some type of limit beyond which I would not proceed. What I found was that the airplane performed equally well*

*throughout the range from GW to GW +40%.*

*So, at Agra, India, we taxied very, very slowly to the runway. I did not let anybody rush me. With all that weight hanging on the wingtips, I did not want to risk overstressing the wing in the slightest. Upon taking the runway, I stated that I would delay the takeoff roll. Again, I did not want to be rushed at all. The idea of rolling onto the runway and continuing the TO roll was rejected because of the inertia and momentum that the heavy wingtips might exert. I decided to do the TO without flaps which is the way I always fly this airplane. Even if an expert could convince me that a partial flap TO was safer, I would reject it because I would be denied the comparison to my normal takeoff feel.*

*I then brought up the power as I held the brakes and as soon as I passed into the yellow TOT (turbine outlet temperature) arc, I released the brakes and set the power at the very top of the yellow. As we rolled, I made **very** slight rudder/nosewheel corrections — very slight. The airplane tracked the center line exactly so I did not have to settle for an angled TO which I was prepared to do rather than risk an abrupt correction which might induce a momentum turn followed by an opposite over correction. At 65 kts, I lightened up ever so slightly on the forward pressure and at 85 kts I let the airplane fly, and as soon as I felt the mains come off the runway, I applied slight forward pressure to gain airspeed. At 95 kts, I let the A/C climb and flew a constant airspeed until I was three wing lengths above the runway (100'). Then, holding forward pressure I let the air speed increase to 100 kts, then pulled up the gear. I flew a 100 kt climb. After five minutes of climb, I pulled the power to the green and leveled the airplane and flew at that altitude for five minutes, then put the power at the top of the yellow again for five minutes. (The engine has a yellow arc limit of five minutes on/five minutes off, etc.)*

*On turns, I limited myself to 1/2 standard rate **and level. No climbing turns.** I continued this restriction until I was down to certified gross weight +15%.*

*Within these parameters of flight everything was normal and quite comfortable.*

*There are things I would not have done:*

1. *Take off into weather other than a smooth stratus layer.*
2. *Take off into any kind of convective or*

*developing convective activity.*

3. *Take off into conditions that might produce the slightest trace of ice.*
4. *Take off into known moderate or greater turbulence.*"

Our departure is at 8:44 a.m. During the long takeoff roll there were some white knuckles in the cockpit (mine), but we are on our way, tracking to the northeast to Farrukhabad (FB) beacon to pick up airway R460 that will take us to Calcutta (CEA). FB to CEA is 534 nautical miles. After Calcutta we will cut across a small corner of Bangladesh's airspace, fly back into the Calcutta Control area, cross the Bay of Bengal, pass over Myanmar (the former Burma) and Thailand, and then do an end run around Kampuchia (Cambodia) over the Gulf of Thailand to our destination, Tansonnhat Airport, Vietnam.

All the piston aircraft and the shorter-range jets will make an interim fueling stop at U-Taphao, a former U.S. Air Force base in Thailand about eighty miles south of Bangkok. The Vietnamese have only Russian avgas and its octane rating is too low for American engines. Their plan is to gas up in U-Taphao, go on to Ho Chi Minh City (Saigon) and, if necessary, top off with the Russian stuff before leaving for Okinawa (mixing in a small amount of lower octane gasoline should be okay). While fueling in U-Taphao all race clocks will stop.

At 13,000 feet the outside air temperature is 25C° (77F°). Haven't they heard of the adiabatic cooling rate in this part of the world? We are over Lucknow (LCK) at 0424 Zulu, only about 100 miles south of the India-Nepal border. I had hopes that maybe we could see the Himalayas from here but it is not to be. There is too much haze. The plains of India roll by below, brown and dry as before. We cross Gaya (GGC) VOR at 0550 Zulu. Now some clouds have formed below us and our view of the ground is becoming obscured. We are about to cross Dhanbad (DB) beacon when another race plane contacts us on our pre-arranged frequency and informs us that the teams ahead are all diverting to the south because Dhaka Control in Bangladesh is warning that any aircraft who enters their airspace will be intercepted and shot down.

Now wait a minute! We're on an international flight plan with an approved clearance. After Calcutta, airway A1 cuts through the southernmost corner of the Dhaka FIR. We'll only be in their airspace for about thirty-seven minutes and we certainly don't intend any mischief while we're there. They can't be serious.

But what if they are? Do we really want to test this one?

"Calcutta Control, this is November 9675 Romeo, Flight Level one three zero. Request clearance from BEGET intersection direct MADAK A349 Bangkok." This routing, slightly to the south, will cost us about forty extra miles but will keep us clear of Dhaka FIR. Calcutta grants the clearance without questions. They have most likely been giving a similar one to every race plane in front of us. Bob passes the message back down the line.

As we near the shoreline of the Bay of Bengal the clouds below get higher with buildups. We are in and out of clouds now. Passing over the Ganges River Delta south of Calcutta I catch glimpses of winding waterways and swampy strips of land. These give way to the waters of the Bay of Bengal, between India and Burma. Four hundred and fifteen miles of open water. That will take us two hours and twenty-two minutes at our present ground speed of 170 knots. It doesn't seem like anything to get excited about anymore. Hell, we've flown the Atlantic, haven't we?

Six and one-half hours from Agra we make landfall over Myanmar. The sun is way past its zenith now. The air temperature is still in the mid-seventies at 13,000 feet. It is over two hours yet to Bangkok. Radio communications are pretty good in this part of the world. We had been given a coded number sequence for our clearance to fly over Myanmar and had no trouble giving it to Yangon (Rangoon) Control. The same is true for our routine position reports. This part of the country is choked with rivers and inlets. I can see occasional houses built on stilts out over the water. The land itself is heavily forested.

The sun is low as we cross Dawei (DWI) VOR and turn left thirty-four degrees toward Bangkok. TANEK intersection is on the border of Thailand and we cross it at 1129 Zulu. Up ahead we can see towering thunderstorms right in our path. Bob's Stormscope, which can locate electrical activity up to several hundred miles away, shows they are active cells. As we get closer to Bangkok and the sky begins to darken we see flashes of lightning in the black clouds.

"Bangkok Center, November 9675 Romeo, be advised we are deviating south of the airway to avoid thunderstorms."

"75 Romeo, roger."

While this is going on I'm doing some quick calculating. By the time we get in the vicinity of Bangkok we will have been in the air for over eight and one-half hours. Tansonnhat, our destination, is 505 nautical miles from Bangkok if we follow the offshore route prescribed on the charts. Cambodia (Kampuchia) is a no-no area for international flights — they seem to be locked in a perpetual civil war and many aeronautical charts have the country's boundaries overlaid with jagged red slashes warning airmen to stay out. But there's an airway, R468, minimum altitude FL80, that runs straight as an arrow between Bangkok and Ho Chi Minh City. It goes right over Cambodia's capital, Phnom Penh. Going that way would save us 102 miles or 36 minutes. If we go the long way around, avoiding Cambodia, it will take another three hours of flying leaving us only about 45 minutes of reserve fuel.

Bob studies the situation while he dodges thunderstorms in the dusk. "Let's try it," he says. "The worse they can say is no. Let's get this flight over as soon as possible."

Bob short-circuits the system, "Bangkok Center, this is November 9675 Romeo, six miles south of Bangkok VOR at flight level 130, estimating Phnom Penh at 1335 Zulu. Tansonnhat next."

"9675 Romeo, roger your position. Do you have authorization to overfly Kampuchia?"

"Affirmative." (a lie)

"What is your authorization number?"

Bob thinks fast when he has to. "Charlie 124 dash 94," he says with the assuring tones of a confidence man.

"75 Romeo, roger. We will verify. Report BOKAK intersection to Phnom Penh on 123.8."

"9675 Romeo. Roger." Now we will see if the bluff works.

We turn southeast into the night sky as I punch in the latitude and longitude of BOKAK intersection, the boundary marker for Cambodia.

At BOKAK Bob dutifully calls Phnom Penh Control several times but receives no answer. Cambodia appears unlit on the ground. There are no lights to be seen anywhere. I try to imagine the jungles and hills we are flying over, and what life must be like for the average working stiff or farmer in this miserable land below. This is the place of the killing fields and the Khymer Rouge. Are they tracking us on radar right now? The transponder shows no flashing "R" so I guess the answer is no. What are the chances they will intercept us in the air? Do they even have an air force with that capability? Do they give a damn if we overfly their country with or without authorization?

The thunderstorms are behind us and we are in smooth air in clear weather. Stars are visible now. Our estimate for Phnom Penh is 1335 Zulu and as we get closer, the city lights appear. It's too early in the evening for city folks to be in bed but the lights are scattered far apart in such a way that I can see no central downtown area. Our course takes us directly over the center of the city. As we pass Phnom Penh VOR (PNH) Bob gives them another call on the radio, but no reply is received again. This is truly turning out to be our stealth mission.

There is more flying over blackness. Thirty minutes after Phnom Penh we are at SAPEN intersection and about to enter the airspace of Vietnam. Tansonnhat Airport is only thirty miles away.

"Tansonnhat, this is November 9675 Romeo. SAPEN at 03, flight level 130, estimating Tansonnhat at 14."

They come right back. "November 9675 Romeo. Roger. Maintain 7,000 feet."

They give us the current altimeter, winds and active runway, and three minutes later, "9675 Romeo, cleared for straight-in approach and landing." No controller says a thing like that unless he is having a very quiet evening.

The airport is easy to spot north of the central part of the city and Bob sets up a long straight approach. The field elevation is only 33 feet. We touch down at 1415 Zulu. The local time is 9:15 p.m. It's a new endurance record for us — eleven hours and one minute in the air.

Three men and two women meet our aircraft as we shut down. There are no welcoming smiles or handshakes. We seem to be near a floodlit fence that forms part of the airport boundary yet we are fairly close to the main passenger terminal. I nod hello to our welcoming committee, point over to a darker section of the fence, and inquire if it would be all right to step over there and relieve myself. (I have not urinated during the entire flight although I have a patented "Littlejohn" bottle with me. It has been so warm that I have sweated out much of my excess moisture, but now nature calls). This request is met with looks of incomprehension. Evidently no one speaks English. I repeat my request, this time in pantomime, and they all get the idea immediately. Laughter breaks out, accompanied by vigorous nodding and waving of arms, to let me know it will be perfectly all right.

We are escorted to the terminal's VIP lounge with large leather overstuffed chairs. Our passports and visas are confiscated and we are each given several forms to fill out — name, address, age, purpose of travel, length of stay, etc. Everyone is very formal. After half and hour we are directed to a waiting van. In it is a young English-speaking woman, kind of dumpy with short straight hair cut in bangs, who announces herself as a Vietnam Government representative who will accompany us to our hotel. On the long ride into town she delivers a stern lecture to us.

"The People's Army liberated Ho Chi Minh City from its oppressors in 1975. Since then we have created a new workers' paradise where all are equal and all prosperous. While you are here you will see the improvements that have been made by the unified government of the People's Republic. Were either of you here during the war? Were you bomber pilots?"

"No," we both say together.

"Good. Our government wishes you a pleasant time while you visit our country. I have some advice to make your stay happy."

We are all ears.

"Do not leave your hotel alone at night. When you are out on the streets keep one hand on your purse all the time because there are many pickpockets. Put your valuables in the hotel safe. Stay away from prostitutes because venereal disease is everywhere. If you want a taxicab, have the clerk at the hotel call one — don't get into one on the street because there are many robbers in the city. Be careful of your passports. Many people like to steal them."

"We haven't got our passports. Your people took them away at the airport."

"You will get them back at the hotel tomorrow. Any other questions?"

We've heard quite enough, thank you.

The "Dragon Lady," as Bob refers to her later, talks at us all the way in and sees us inside our hotel. The van we came in had no markings so I don't know if it was supplied by Bernard, the hotel or the People's Republic. At least there was no charge.

Saigon still exists. It is now a district of Ho Chi Minh City, and our hotel, The Palace, is in the middle of it. The small lobby is crowded with Europeans, mostly French. I have a short chat with an elderly couple. They are here on holiday, they tell me, because they were born and raised here in the 1920s and '30s. They are visiting their home town.

We get our keys and carry our own bags to our room on the fourth floor. The room is small and third-rate, with two single beds and a narrow bathroom with an old-fashioned tub standing on lion paw legs. This will be our home for the next three nights. I can imagine a hooker turning a trick with some G.I. in here twenty-five years ago. A television set sits on the dresser. It was already turned on when we came in but the screen is only snow. I flip the channels but get nothing. There's no "off" switch I can find and the power cord runs right into the wall so there's no way to unplug it. This TV set will remain a mystery to us all during our stay. It's hot and humid in Saigon but a cranky window air conditioner gives us some relief.

Both of us are tired out from the heat, the long flight and the Dragon Lady. We find the hotel's rooftop restaurant, have a good Chinese meal, and hit the sack early.

THURSDAY, 12 MAY. The morning dawns hot and clear in Saigon. Bob and I are up fairly early and spend some time at our room's open window watching the action on the streets. There seem to be a number of what we Americans call homeless people out there. Some are still sleeping in shop doorways, others are stirring about. Some eat breakfast squatting on the sidewalk. Others, just rising, urinate against skinny little trees planted along the curb. Kiosks in the middle of the broad street are opening up to sell food and merchandise. The avenue is jammed with morning traffic. There are very few cars or trucks. Most of the city is on two wheels. Bicycles, motor bicycles, scooters, and motorcycles make up ninety percent of the traffic. Unconcerned pedestrians weave in and out among them as they make their way across the street.

At breakfast we join some of the other race teams and learn of the near disaster that many of them met at U-Taphao, Thailand.

The gasoline burners had to stop there to fill up with 100-octane low-lead before coming on to Vietnam. Their race clocks were stopped while they went about refueling. Many of them were feeling ill by the time they arrived, most likely from something they had picked up from one of our feasts in India.

*A merchant's food cart in Ho Chi Minh City, Vietnam.*

About half of them became hors de combat from diarrhea and severe nausea. Dr. Willie Tashima, who with admirable foresight had brought a stocked medical kit in his Bonanza, became much in demand professionally. To make matters worse the U-Taphao airport personnel and equipment were not up to the challenge of fueling multiple aircraft in a short time. The airport, a former U.S. Air Force base, was thrown into confusion and long delays in the sweltering heat resulted. Some crew members were too ill to go on and checked into a local hotel which by all reports was a real pesthole. Others, desperate to leave but not sure they were in good enough shape to fly the remaining leg to Tansonnhat, borrowed pilots from the Arc en Ciel organization and the *Tiger* crew to come along with them in case they suffered a relapse in the air. As of this morning, some had yet to arrive in Saigon, some are sick in their hotel beds upstairs, and the ones we are having breakfast with are more or less ready for duty.

Bob has been taking two tetracycline tablets a day since San Diego. I have been taking them too, except now I am on the prescribed doxycycline, a close cousin to tetracycline, for malaria prevention. These prophylactic measures have evidently paid off. Both of us are feeling fine.

Arc en Ciel has laid on a bus tour of the city for us this morning. Because of illness the group getting on the bus is small. We visit the National Museum first and I take Bob's picture at a large bust of Ho Chi Minh in the main rotunda. The museum is dark inside

*Local traffic in Ho Chi Minh City.*

*An enormous bust of Ho Chi Minh.*

and stiflingly hot. The exhibits, while many of the carvings and jewelry pieces are exquisite, are poorly presented or displayed in their glass cases.

After, the bus heads for Chinatown. On our way I am fascinated by the thousands of small shops that line the streets. They are just a few feet wide and extend maybe ten feet back from the sidewalk. They share a wall with the shop next door. Typically, the proprietor is sitting in front under an umbrella. They are highly specialized. This one sells only toys; that one, baskets; and so on. One shop we pass is crammed with nothing but garden hoses.

On our way to Chinatown our Vietnamese guide takes it upon himself to explain all about the Chinese to us. It becomes a kind of racial tirade as he condemns the Chinese for their money-grubbing ways and lack of interest in the arts and sciences. "All they think about," he goes on, "is setting each other up in business while ignoring education and the professions." What the hell is this? Is this personal with him or is he paid to excoriate his nation's largest minority? Moreover, why subject a bunch of innocent tourists to this kind of crap?

We visit a Buddhist Temple in Chinatown and head back downtown. The bus stops at the former American Embassy so we can take photographs. The large square white building sits alone behind its walls and padlocked gates unoccupied. The grounds have been all dug up for some reason (buried treasure?). It's hard to keep the images of 1975 out of one's mind with the crowds all around and helicopters evacuating people from the rooftop.

We have a group lunch with Vietnamese food at a fancy restaurant. Bob and I decline the evening's press conference and dinner cruise on the river. We head back to the hotel for a nap. The long hours in the air and the various strains of this journey are taking their toll and rest is important.

*The decorative entrance to a Chinese temple in Ho Chi Minh City.*

*Ken Johnson and Author at the former U.S. Embassy in Saigon.*

*A wider view of the former U.S. Embassy.*

FRIDAY, 13 MAY. There's a boat trip to the Mekong Delta scheduled for this morning but Bob won't go. He's very prone to seasickness and avoids anything that floats. It's strange, he's never been air-sick in his life, even in the roughest turbulence, but he can't take boats. Instead, we ask the hotel to arrange a car and driver to take us to the airport. When we arrived at the hotel Wednesday night Bob noticed a smear of oil on his sleeve. It may have come from an instrument leak in the cockpit and if that is so, we want to find and repair it now and here, not over the South China Sea tomorrow. The car comes and picks us up. There are two people in it. One drives and the other, riding shotgun, speaks a little English. Forty minutes later we are at the air-craft while the car and its crew wait for us under a tree in the parking lot.

In the broiling sun Bob removes the entire instrument panel cover. We inspect each component carefully, especially the engine instruments, but can find nothing amiss. Everything is dry and secure. After the cover is reinstalled Bob decides we might as well fuel up while we are here and be ready for tomorrow's start. A fuel truck is called for and five or six airport officials arrive on the scene. While Bob is supervising the complications of fueling (we have five different fuel ports) a very small female airport official is waving some forms in my face.

"You pay now," she demands in English.

"We can't. We don't know how much fuel it will take."

"You pay now!" she demands stridently.

"Look lady, it's a nine-hour trip to Okinawa tomorrow and we want to fill the airplane. When it's

*Inside a Buddhist Temple in the Chinatown section of Ho Chi Minh City.*

*Typical farmland in Vietnam.*

full then we'll know how much to pay."

I can see she doesn't understand me. I wave over one of the other officials and while he doesn't speak English either, he gets this "Tiny Terror" to back off and calm down.

Once the fueling is done, the amount, in liters, is fed into the beads of an abacus and a few clicks later the bill is presented. Jet fuel here is about $1.35 a gallon, cheaper than back home, but the amount in the local currency, dongs, is astronomic — about two million, four hundred thousand. Let's see, that's about $337. Bob pays them $350 in U.S. currency and it's smiles all around. No change is offered or expected.

On the ride back to the hotel we pass several war memorials displaying U.S. tanks, aircraft, and other equipment on permanent display. To many Americans the Vietnam War is a fading unhappy memory. To these people it is a fact of everyday life, even a celebration if you are a good Communist. We pass a Catholic Cathedral. It is locked up.

When we return to the Palace Hotel the staff helps us with paying the hired car. The bill for the car, driver, and interpreter for four hours comes to eleven dollars.

In the evening our group at the Palace is bused over to the Majestic Hotel where the rest of the crews are staying. A big dinner is held with entertainment provided by a dance group in elaborate native costumes.

Ken Johnson has had an exciting day. While disem-barking from the Mekong Delta cruise he was jostled by several Vietnamese teens and a moment later realized his passport had been stolen. He had carelessly been carrying it in an outside pocket. Back at the hotel and worried sick about it (the U.S. has no consulate in Ho Chi Minh City), he received a telephone call telling him he could buy his passport back just across the street from the hotel entrance if he came alone. He went out, in the dark, and spotted a group of teenagers, one of whom was holding his passport and waving it at him. Ken approached him holding a twenty dollar bill in his left hand and without a word snatched his passport away while the thief grabbed the twenty. Ken spun around and started sprinting for the hotel. The gang gave chase but Ken is in good shape and beat them back. That ended the incident.

Bob and I both express our opinion to Ken that he is one lucky tourist — not only to get his passport back for only twenty dollars, but to still be alive and in one piece.

Bob has written some of his thoughts about our visit to Ho Chi Minh City:

*It's my first visit back to Saigon since 1963. The war is over and the purveyors of the communist credo have won the day. Our guide, "The Dragon Lady," spouts socialist propaganda to us nonstop during the ride from the airport to the hotel. We are told (instructed) about the great victory of the North over the South and the defeat of the American Imperialist Forces. Central planning and collectivism have conquered capitalism and have created a new workers' paradise.*

*Next morning we arise early and view the scene*

*The "Tiger" stands out at Tonsonnhat Airport in Ho Chi Minh City.*

*unfolding in the square beneath our shabby hotel window. Street urchins rise from their sidewalk beds and urinate in the streets. I still remember yesterday's lecture about their workers' paradise. Then an Army truck appears. There is a confrontation with young men. They are beaten and thrown into the truck, along with their motorcycles. We had been warned that it was not safe to wander about. Are these the criminals?*

*On our tour of Saigon's Chinatown, we are made to view the Chinese as if they are animals in the zoo. The tour guide spouts a litany. "These are Chinese — they are money-grubbing, selfish people. They are filthy capitalists. They are not quite human, they are illiterate." The world, it seems to me, has heard this kind of litany against a people before. More than troubling.*

*The bus finally stops in front of a Buddhist Temple. I go in and light three incense sticks for the Chinese "untermen."*

*As we drive back to the hotel, I feel rage at the thoughts of Jane Fonda and her escapades during the Vietnam War. I finally calmed as the skies opened with a thankful downpour, cleaning the streets of urine and feces, wondering Ms. Fonda's real thoughts and behavior if she lived here, without privilege, in this workers' paradise. Oh, for the sake of all who live and hope here, how I wish that this were true — that it were a workers' paradise.*

## FLASHBACK VIII

## "CRASH COURSE"

**DECEMBER 1955.** The monthly "Fly Safe" meeting was entering its second hour in the rooms of the 84th Air Transport Squadron (Heavy) at Travis AFB. The Squadron Safety officer, Major Logan, had covered a few recent CAA rule changes, some technical modifications on the C-124's they all flew, and had read the latest Air Force accident summaries. He could see from the bored expressions and the frequent glances at wristwatches that he was losing his audience. He decided to wind it up.

"One last thing, gentlemen. We have been remiss in our emergency procedures training. Regulations require all crew members to annually practice emergency ground evacuation from the airplane. Accordingly, I have had a Globemaster towed over on the ramp outside and we will now practice using the escape chute."

With groans and muttering all around, the men assembled on the ramp by the aircraft and watched the escape chute being deployed. It was not the automatic inflatable chute of today, but a simple five foot wide sheet of heavy nylon hung from the aft elevator door at a 45 degree angle to the ground and anchored by two husky airmen straining at the other end 25 feet away.

Everyone took his turn sliding down. Some of the junior officers had never done it before and found it kind of fun — like being at an amusement park. The drill over, the senior officers wandered off in search of coffee. One Lieutenant (our hero) said to another, "I'll bet if I got up a little speed, I could land almost halfway down that chute!" Then he went ahead and proved he could. It caught on fast. Within five minutes young pilots and navigators were running the entire length of the airplane's cargo deck, hitting their mark at the elevator doors like Olympic long-jumpers, and sailing out into space to land on the last third of the escape chute. "Yahoo," they shouted as they leapt. Bets were being placed.

Major Logan, who had been called to the phone, stepped out of the offices just in time to see a 2nd Lieutenant fly out, land too far over on the edge of the chute, rebound 90 degrees to the right, and with arms and legs flailing hit the cement ramp with a sickening thud. He lay there unmoving.

Later, it was learned his injuries were only a concussion and a broken collar bone. There was no mention of the incident at future safety meetings, and the drill was never repeated.

# CHAPTER 9

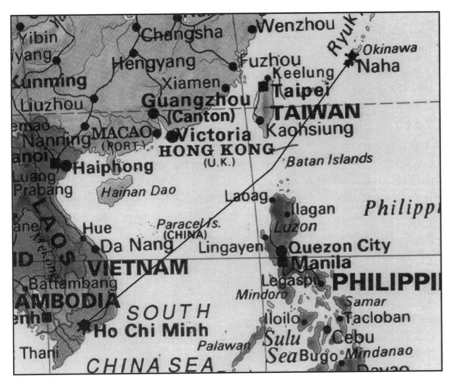

# SAIGON

# TO

# NAHA

SATURDAY, 14 MAY. The local time is 3:30 p.m. It's a classic south seas afternoon as we cruise along at 11,000 feet. Puffy scattered fair weather cumulus clouds stretch from horizon to horizon and the atmosphere is so clear you can see forever. The air is smooth and although the winds are costing us almost twenty knots of ground speed, that's no worry because we have plenty of fuel. A kind of peacefulness pervades the cockpit. Bob and I are silent most of the time as we gaze out the windows. I'm thinking back almost forty years when I spent many an afternoon like this, in an Air Force transport over the Western Pacific on a beautiful day, heading for some exotic destination.

We are nearing SEKSI intersection, a point in the South China Sea at least 300 miles from the nearest land based VOR. The GPS is working fine now that I take care to turn it on at the right time. It's been an hour and forty minutes since our last compulsory reporting point, and we still have a long way to go. Our route today is over the South China Sea,

through the Luzon Strait between the Philippines and Taiwan, and over part of the Philippine Sea to the Ryukyu Islands and our destination, Naha Airport on the island of Okinawa. Although we will never be more than a few hundred miles from land, it will be the longest over-water leg of the entire trip.

Our day did not start out as smoothly as this afternoon's tranquil ambience would lead you to believe. We all got to the airport early in anticipation of another long day's flight. Mercifully, our members who were ill now seem to be recovered fully, thanks to tetracycline and penicillin. The first glitch came when it was announced that all our filed flight plans were now invalid and would have to be done over. All aircraft had requested the most direct route between Vietnam and Okinawa but word had just been received that both the Hong Kong and Taiwan authorities didn't want us in their airspace, not even if we were just going to overfly a portion of it. First Saudi Arabia, then Bangladesh, and now Taiwan and Hong Kong have arbitrarily decided they would just rather not be bothered with us. Never mind that denying their airspace will cause us to fly a couple of hundred extra miles as we route around them. There's nothing to be done. If you tried to appeal a decision like this you would spend the next several days on the telephone and probably lose anyway.

Along with the others, I raced over to Operations, replotted a course to avoid the forbidden areas, refigured the time en route, and filled out all the other information blocks. All of this took most of an hour. Then back to the aircraft and let's get out of here.

But no, Bangkok Control, which handles the airspace all around Vietnam, had refused departure clearances. No explanation was forthcoming. It was 92 degrees in the shade and getting hotter. We stood around by the planes for two hours in the hot sun wondering if we would ever be allowed to escape. It wasn't traffic in or out of Tansonnhat that caused the delay — there was almost none.

Finally, the aircraft were allowed to start departing. We got our clearance and Bob started the take-off roll at 11:21 a.m. (0621 Zulu). Damn! Almost half the daylight hours wasted again. There's got to be a better system than this. Now we will have a long flight after sunset and a night arrival in Okinawa.

For eighty-five miles we flew east over the heavy jungle and occasional farming areas of Vietnam until Phanthiet VOR which is on the coastline. It's all water from here on, 1,450 miles of it.

Now, five hours into the flight our Vietnamese frustrations are a thing of the past. Bob has his thermos of coffee and I my bottled water. The Bonanza is performing in its usual perfect way. The ocean is bright blue below us and the cloud shadows are lengthening as the day begins to end.

"Robert, my man," I say, "you're in for a real treat. You're going to see one spectacular sunset. Pay attention, because in these latitudes they don't last long."

My forecast turns out to be true. There are some cumulus buildups to the west this afternoon and as the sun goes behind them the rays are refracted outwards in huge golden fan patterns. The blood red light of the horizon gives way to dark purple as the sun goes below the earth's rim. God's kinetic painting has transfixed us for one memorable hour. We still have almost four hours to go, now in pitch dark.

I have always found flying over the ocean at night to be rather tedious. Without a big moon or sky full of stars, there's nothing to look at. You check the engine instruments to make sure all is normal, check to see you are holding the proper course and that your estimate for the next reporting point still looks good, sit there a minute or two, and then do it all over again. Time drags slowly. Tonight we're fighting headwinds all the way to Okinawa. My original estimate for time en route, based on the winds aloft forecast back in Ho Chi Minh City, was for eight hours, fifty minutes, but these winds are stronger than that. It looks like nine and a half at least. At NIKET intersection we turn more eastward to avoid the Taipei FIR and head direct for MEVIN intersection, passing about 100 miles north of Laoag, the northernmost point in the Philippines. At MEVIN we will be 428 miles from our destination.

We pass MEVIN and SADEK and our estimate for Miyakojima VOR (MYC) is 1324 Zulu. Miyakojima is in the Ryukyu Islands and therefore belongs to Japan. Now we're getting someplace.

The radio is picking up a one-sided conversation on the race frequency. We can't hear the second aircraft but the one we do hear is Dr. Willie Tashima and Herb Halperin in their Bonanza. They departed over an hour ahead of us this morning and we are finally catching up to them.

"Hey, Willie, this is Bob and Dennis. How ya doin?"

"Bob! Fine, ol' buddy. We're down here at nine thousand about twenty minutes past Miyakojima. Where are you?"

They go on in this vein for awhile. Some quick calculations show that we will overtake them about ten minutes from Naha. Unlike us, Willie and Herb are still racing seriously. They are lagging behind in the standings in their class, but they are still game.

Bob makes them a most gallant offer.

"Look, Willie, when we get in contact with Naha Approach, I'll request a delay so you can land first. That way you'll save a few minutes on the clock."

"Thanks, Bob. Much appreciated."

We pass Miyakojima and start the last leg of the trip toward Naha. After some time we spot a rotating beacon up ahead and below us. It's framed by red and green wingtip lights. We are slowly overtaking them.

"Willie, this is Bob. We have you in sight. We'll

pass above you and to your left."

Fifty miles out we are talking to Approach Control. The voice on the ground is American. We have a large Air Force base, Kadena, near Naha, and the USAF evidently handles arrivals and departures for both. Bob explains what we want to do and the controller comprehends the situation immediately.

"Roger, 75 Romeo, cross Naha VOR at eleven thousand and descend to five thousand on heading three two zero."

We come in right over the city. The weather is clear. We head out to sea again on 320 degrees and Bob starts a descent. I'm not particularly keen about flying low over water at night and it

*The Manza Beach Hotel and grounds at Okinawa.*

seems we are halfway to Korea before the controller gets through with Willie and vectors us back onto the approach path.

We land at 11:23 p.m. local time (1423 Zulu). Our flight from Ho Chi Minh City, what with the winds and our deferring to Dr. Tashima, has taken ten hours and two minutes.

We are through Customs and Immigration in a snap. A taxi waits for us outside the quiet terminal, The driver has a chit which he will cash in at the hotel when we arrive. Bob and I know the name of our quarters for the next two days, the Manza Beach Hotel, but we have no idea where it is. The taxi goes through the Naha downtown area. Bob is amazed. He served eighteen months on Okinawa in the 1960s and Naha was a fairly simple place. Now it's all sky-

scrapers and freeways. Since the islands reverted to Japan from U.S. administration in 1974 the Japanese have evidently poured a ton of money into development.

Once we leave Naha we have a long ride in the country, passing through occasional villages. Bernard had mentioned some time ago that taxi fare from the airport to the hotel would exceed $100, but I had dismissed it as an exaggeration. But this ride, about ninety minutes long, would cost at least a hundred dollars back in the States.

*Bob Reiss relaxing near a spectacular view from the Manza Beach Hotel grounds.*

We finally arrive. The Manza Beach Hotel is a magnificent resort. The hotel itself rises ten stories high with the upper floors ringing the lobby whose open space extends from ground level to the roof. Our keys are waiting. The room is ultra modern. The hotel has put two cold meals of sandwiches, fruit and pastries on the table. We tuck into these gratefully before going to bed.

SUNDAY, 15 MAY. We have a great breakfast in the dining room. The Manza Beach Hotel is a complete vacation resort with at least a square mile of grounds. It has its own private beach, a yacht basin, hiking trails and golf course. It occupies a section of the west coast of the island where the lava stone cliffs have been shaped into surrealistic forms by the constant surf. The other guests, almost all Japanese,

seem to be made up of a good percentage of honeymooners. I've been told the rooms go for close to $400 a day and I believe it.

Bob was stationed on this island during the early 1960s when he was an Army Intelligence agent working at Camp Torii. I have been here, too, but never for more than a day or so. After breakfast Bob joins a group of fellow racers for a bus tour of native Okinawan life. I pass, and spend the morning resting and doing a hand laundry in the room. By midday our balcony, overlooking the large hotel pool, is festooned with drying socks, shorts and shirts.

Bob returns from his tour with a prize. He has bought several bottles of the local moonshine (rice whiskey) that contain a dead viper pickled in the liquor. The snakes called "Habu Habu" are native to the islands, and have the squarish heads common to many poisonous reptiles. They are nasty looking critters, about a foot long, and certainly outclass the worm in a Mexican tequila bottle. He will take the bottles back to San Diego as gifts for friends.

In the evening Bernard holds his usual, and to us by now boring, press conference and this is followed by one whale of a dinner and reception by the local leading citizens in a private room. The Vice Governor of Okinawa Prefecture is there and graciously welcomes us. The fact that she is female further reinforces my impression that a lot of changes have been made in the last twenty-four years since I lived in Japan. Dinner is a standup affair with heavy hors d'oeuvres and lots of booze. The formalities over, a troop of dancers are brought on for our entertainment. The females are in kimonos and the males are dressed outlandishly in rice straw skirts with whitened faces, raccoon-like blackened eyes, and dayglow fright wigs. Each male carries a large drum to accompany the dancing. The show lasts an hour. The gyrations of the dancers are frantic, and the noise is deafening. I lived in Japan for three years in the 60s and thought I knew the culture fairly well, but I've never seen anything like this.

MONDAY, 16 MAY. We will not depart Okinawa until tomorrow, but this morning all crews are bused to the airport so we can fuel the aircraft and file our flight plans. Trouble develops right off. The Japanese authorities won't let us beyond an anteroom in the terminal and can't seem to give an adequate reason for the delay. Naha International is a joint-use airport where the Japanese Air Self-Defense Force has on operating base and I suspect there is some security concern that is keeping us off the ramp and away from our airplanes. Bernard, speaking through an interpreter, demands immediate access and when this is denied, both he and several other of his French assistants begin shouting, threatening, and generally carrying on like spoiled jerks. (Careful, Bernard. I know the Japanese. You can push them only so far while they remain stoic and implacable, and then just like in a samurai movie, some tiny switch will flick from "off" to "berserk" and then there will be hell to pay.) The Japanese officials end this dramatic scene by simply walking away.

When we finally gain entry to the ramp we see that the airport has only made one gasoline and one jet fuel truck available for all seventeen aircraft. It's going to be a long morning. It's a clear but hazy day and it's also going to be hot. Some tinker with their airplanes, others simply seek out some shade under the wings. Our only diversion is watching the landings and takeoffs of the Japanese F-4 Phantom fighters.

We had learned yesterday that the two Norwegians, Poju Stephansen and Jan Roang, had an emergency during their arrival here. As they neared the airport they were cleared to begin their descent. When they reduced power the oil pressure on the single engine of their Cessna 210 fell to zero. They declared an emergency and were cleared straight in. The engine kept running and they landed without incident. After shutdown they found the oil level to be quite low but there was no evidence of a broken line or a leak. Now, out on the ramp, they pull the oil filter and split it open. Those of us standing by can see that it is totally clogged with a tar-like goop that looks like melted plastic. They have been using Mobil I synthetic oil in their crankcase during the entire race so far and neither they nor any of us know enough about synthetic oil to even guess what went wrong. One of the major concerns is to find out if there are any metal pieces in the residue. Someone finds an ordinary housepin and this is used to puncture the little platelets stuck in the filter. They seem to be made of carbon, with no metal at their cores. The local Japanese repair facility does not have a microscope, so a closer look cannot be made.

Bob suggests they fill the crankcase with some locally available 40-weight regular oil, run up the engine, drain it again, and then if everything looks okay, fill the crankcase with 50-weight oil, put in a fresh filter, and go with that. This is what they do and everything seems to check out fine.

After three hours of waiting, a fuel truck finally pulls up to the Bonanza. We have just started the process of filling the aircraft when one of Bernard's team, the one Bob calls "the Kraut," appears and tells us to stop everything and come attend an emergency meeting that Lamy has called for in the terminal. Everyone must attend.

"No," says Bob. "We've finally got the truck and I don't want him to get away. Dennis can go. I'll stay here and see to the fueling."

"Bernard wants everyone. You must come. We insist."

Bob is not overly fond of Frenchmen to begin with, especially those who are officious and tell him what he "must" do. In his hand he is holding the large screwdriver we use to remove the auxiliary tank cap.

"Get away from me you son-of-a-bitch," he says in a way that causes the Frenchman to start eyeballing the screwdriver and backing away.

"I am just passing on a message," he says, and leaves.

I make it to the meeting. It's no big deal. The Japanese ATC authorities have decided we must all take a different route to Sendai from the one they had specified before. It's simply a matter of refiling our flight plans, a routine exercise by now on our trip.

Fueling over and our flight plan redone, we have had enough of this scene and decide to go off on our own. It's about 1:00 p.m. and I offer to take Bob to lunch at the Kadena AFB Officers' Club. We take a cab from the airport and get over to the base only to find the O' Club doesn't serve lunch anymore.

Traditionally, O' Clubs have lost money on their food service and made it up on bar sales. Now, with the service-wide crackdown on alcoholism, the serious drinkers, always the mainstay of club economics, avoid being seen imbibing in public and the clubs have had to retrench. We find a Pizza Hut franchise on the base and eat there instead. It's astonishing how good familiar food tastes when you've been away for awhile.

Another cab takes us up into the hills to Camp Torii where Bob was based thirty years ago. To my surprise we are able to gain access to the base, cab and all, on the strength of my retired reserve officer's ID card. Bob conducts me on a nostalgic tour of the camp where he worked as a Chinese language interpreter in the intelligence center buried deep underground here.

After the long (and expensive) ride back to the hotel we are treated to a terrific cook-your-own-at-the-table barbecue dinner in the dining room. We have a 0430 call in the morning for the flight to Sendai, a city on the east coast of Japan just over a hundred miles north of Tokyo.

## FLASHBACK IX

## "GAS ATTACK"

JANUARY 1956. Our hero, still a junior copilot on C-124 Globemasters, was on a crew that had just landed at Honolulu International. The trip from Wake Island had been routine and now he looked forward to fifteen hours of ground time and some sleep before departure tomorrow for the mainland and home. After the aircraft had parked and shut down it was his duty to stay in the cockpit and fill out the aircraft's flight logs plus note any "squawks" for the maintenance people. While he was about this task the rest of the crew was down on the cargo deck quickly changing from flight suits to class A uniforms. Changing clothes was not their idea but was done only because Lt. General Joseph Smith, Commander of the Military Air Transport Service in Washington, had ordered it. The General thought it would be good for crew morale to board and depart all MATS aircraft wearing uniform and tie. (Note: the General was dead wrong about this.)

As this was going on, a civilian in coveralls with the logo "US Dept. of Agriculture" approached. He carried a yellow canister about the size of a pineapple. It was marked "DDT." His job was to meet all aircraft arriving from overseas and make sure no foreign bugs contaminated American shores. He stuck his head into the nose wheel door hatch.

"Anybody still in there?"

"Just me," answered our hero, pulling on his pants. "Be right out."

"Look Mac, I've got to start fumigating within ten minutes after arrival and you've been here eleven already. That's it." He pulled the pin on the canister, threw it inside, and slammed the door. Within seconds the aircraft was filled with dense yellow choking fumes.

The Lieutenant, half dressed and gagging on the acrid fumes, groped his way to one of the side portholes. Through watering eyes he could see the rest of the crew waving cheerfully from the ramp.

After fifteen minutes of this the Agriculture man opened the aircraft and let him out. His dizziness and nausea lasted only about two hours. On future flights he was a lot faster deplaning at Honolulu.

# CHAPTER 10

# NAHA

# TO

# SENDAI

TUESDAY, 17 MAY.  It's 10:30 in the morning and we are at 11,000 feet as we fly up the chain of the Ryukyu Islands.  Our course is set for Kagoshima on the island of Kyushu, the southernmost of the home islands of Japan.  It's a great day.  Visibility is a little restricted by haze but the skies are clear and the winds on our tail are giving us a twenty-two knot boost.  To our left is the East China Sea and over to the east lies the Philippine Sea.  Many of the small islands we are passing over are volcanic mountain peaks sticking up through the ocean's surface.  Quite a few are active.  Thin smoke comes out of their craters giving me the impression that Reiss and Stewart, two American city boys, are a long way from home.

Our departure this morning was handled well by the Japanese air traffic control system.  All fueled up the day before, we were spared the uncertainties that usually go with that process.  ATC had decided to route us along the west coast of Japan's main islands and thereby keep us as far away as practicable from the busy Tokyo area.  We took off at 9:01 a.m. Japan time (0001 Zulu) and since the distance to Sendai is only 1,027 nautical miles, we should complete the entire leg in full daylight, a welcome change.  Because of the relatively shorter distance, we are carrying only about eight hours of fuel, so the take-off was shorter than usual and our climb faster.

A little over two hours from departure we make landfall at Kagoshima.  There are broken clouds below us now but the day is better than I expected.  May is the month of the Japanese "Subai" or rainy season, the annual drenching of these islands that makes possible the growth of two rice crops a year.  The season is not one of storms, but rather of almost daily clouds and showers.  Over a hundred million people live on these four main islands that in total area are about equal to Montana.  They tend to crowd up in cities along the coasts where the land is flatter.  The interior is mostly mountainous.  As always, the surface terrain is green and well tended.

Now, over the home islands, we are under radar

monitoring and position reports are no longer necessary. The Japanese controllers speak fluent English and I suspect Tokyo Air Traffic Control Center has detailed their best linguists to the sectors through which we are passing. It's really like flying back in the States.

At Oita we leave Kyushu and cross the Bungo Strait to the island of Shikoku. The clouds reach higher and are more dense now. We begin flying through the taller buildups but there is little turbulence. When over Takamatzu VOR (TZC) we make a 75-degree turn to the left for a short crossing of the Inland Sea to the main island of Honshu, turn northeast again at Okayama, and proceed over to the west coast of Japan. Soon the Sea of Japan is visible. Over Wakasa Bay the clouds begin to thin out and the weather improves.

I can see a lot on the ground now. When I lived in Japan, 1967-1970, I did quite a bit of traveling, both on Navy business and for pleasure, but never got to this part of the country. It is mountainous, as one would expect, and even in mid-May the peaks are snowcapped. There are numerous towns and villages along the coast and behind them, up in the hills, we begin to see some luxury resorts. Each one is a large modern hotel surrounded by at least one full-size golf course. Many have two or even three courses. They have been carved out of the hills to satisfy the Japanese national passion for the game. I'll bet the bill for a week at one of these establishments would be a real heart-stopper.

At Niigata we leave the Sea of Japan and begin the last leg of our flight which is across the narrow part of Honshu to the Pacific side of the island. The weather is absolutely clear as we cross the 86 nautical miles of mountainous terrain.

Sendai is one of the major cities of northern Honshu. It is an administrative and railway center for this part of the country. During World War II it was also the home of the elite Sendai Marines. Because of its importance it was one of many large Japanese cities that were targeted by the 20th Air Force and subsequently utterly destroyed by B-29 Superfortress raids. Virtually nothing we shall see in the city will be over fifty years old.

Sendai airport is easy to spot on this clear beau-

*The racers arrival at Sendai, Japan.*

*A curious onlooking couple watch the Author retrieve some luggage upon arrival at Sendai.*

tiful day. We are cleared for a visual approach and Bob greases it on for the perfect ending to a perfect flight. Our arrival time is 2:18 p.m. (0518 Zulu), after five hours, seventeen minutes in the air from Okinawa.

The tower directs us to the race parking area. As we taxi over we see the area is crowded with people, and a ground handler signals us to shut down outside. At least a thousand of Sendai's citizens are here to greet the race crews on this Tuesday afternoon. Small general aviation aircraft are virtually unknown in Japan and it is apparent that we are generating lots of interest. We hand push the Bonanza through the crowd to its assigned spot while scores of eager hands help us. Everyone is smiling as they greet us. It's a hero's welcome. This is more like it — so much better than arriving at some deserted airport at two o'clock in the morning.

Later Bob fuels the plane for our flight to Kamchatka the day after tomorrow. When he makes to pay the fuelers we are told that the bill will be sent to the hotel and it can be paid before we depart on Thursday. Think of it, a place where pilots are actually trusted to pay their debts honestly, and not try to sneak the aircraft out without paying! Japan is different from the rest of the world.

The Sendai Kokusai Hotel is ultra modern and right downtown. On the bus ride into the city my thoughts returned to those three years when I lived among these people. They were three wonderful yet frustrating years as I struggled to learn the language (much of it forgotten now) and risked my life daily behind the wheel of my Nissan Cedric in some of the world's worst traffic. I was Director of Civilian Training at the Yokosuka Naval Base, about 60 miles south of Tokyo, and my family and I lived in a Japanese house in a beach town called Hayama. My staff of twenty-four Japanese at work seemed amusingly inefficient now and then, but at the same time as effective as any group with whom I had ever worked. As a manager all I had to do was describe what I wanted and when I wanted it, and then stay out of their way. The average Japanese knows more about group dynamics and effectiveness at the age of seven than most Americans learn in a lifetime. My staff gently trained me in their ways for those three years and made me, I think, a better manager.

Now, looking out of the bus window, I searched for changes in the twenty-four years since I left. The school children in their neat uniforms still looked healthy, alert, and as well behaved as always. The general tempo of life was as I remembered. You rarely see anyone doing nothing in public. Everyone is either working or purposely going somewhere. If anything, the people are better dressed than I remember.

My real cultural shock came when I went up to the hotel desk to change some dollars into yen. Yes, I knew in advance that the exchange rate has dropped over the years to about a hundred yen to the dollar from the three hundred and sixty exchange rate of the 60s, but when my fifty dollar bill brings me only 5,000 yen in return, I gulp. To my old way of thinking 5,000 yen is $13.89! Back in Okinawa we had not bothered to change any money since dollars seemed acceptable wherever we went. But here I was going to get a new lesson in economics. Other members of our group were already being educated too. At the airport Dr. Willie Tashima had noticed his nosewheel looked a bit low and requested some air. A mechanic had pumped up the tire and the fixed base operator had presented him with a bill for fifty

*Downtown Sendai*

*Part of the group excursion at Matsushima Bay about 90 minutes from Sendai.*

*Scenic rock shoreline near Matsushima.*

dollars!

In the evening several of us are in the hotel bar watching Dr. Willie teach the bartender how to make the perfect dry martini (at $11.00 each) when we are approached by a member of the local press and asked for an interview. We oblige and all of us bask in this celebrity treatment for half an hour. Later we are the guests of honor at a buffet dinner held in a private meeting room upstairs. Our hosts are the business and civic leaders of Sendai. They are a prosperous looking group in their expensive suits.

Conversation with them is limited to the availability of the two female interpreters present in the room. (Most Japanese executives avoid becoming fluent in a foreign language when they are starting their careers. English, especially, is a difficult language to learn and those who master it risk being sidetracked into becoming interpreters, a low-paying profession.) The executives do throw a nice party though.

*Some of the racers walking at Matsushima.*

*Drummers entertaining passersby in Matsushima Park.*

WEDNESDAY, 18 MAY. This morning we all played tourist. Arc en Ciel had hired a large bus and we all went for a visit to Matsushima Bay about ninety minutes north of Sendai. The bay has hundreds of picturesque pine-covered islands and the nearby park holds a grove of stately trees reported to be sacred. It's a great tourist center and on this cool but bright day we enjoy the sights along with the crowds of Japanese. In the park our guide points out the numerous caves in the cliffs where once Buddhist ascetics made their homes, and in more recent times the local citizenry sought shelter from American bombers.

For lunch we were taken to a large classically Japanese house situated in a corner of the park. Outside, on the grounds, there was a demonstration of Japanese drumming. Six musicians flailed away in the intricate rhythms on various size drums, one of them as big as a Volkswagen. What is it with these drums? When I lived here before, I attended many functions and traveled all over, but never saw a demonstration of drumming. Is this something new for tourists?

Lunch was held upstairs sitting on the floor at long low tables. Our local hosts wanted to give us the experience of a typical Japanese meal yet were fully sensitive to the prejudices of the Western palate ("My God! Is that fish raw?"), so they compromised by serving us cold hamburger steak as the main course. It was awful.

After our return to the city I decided to take a lone walk around town. As is so easy for foreigners in a

*Left:*

*Ken Johnson and Larry Cioppi in Matsushima Park.*

*Below:*

*Dawn Bartsch and Bob Reiss in Matsushima Park. The Bartschs, Bob and the Author also went on the 1992 World Flight, as did Dr. Wilford Tashima.*

Japanese city, I became lost in short order and found myself having to ask directions back to the hotel. I popped into a small tobacco shop and dredged up what Japanese I could manage.

"Ahno ne, Sendai Kokusai Hoteru wa, doko desu ka, kudasai." ("Ahem. Sendai Kokusai Hotel, as for, where is, verbal question mark, please hand down.)

The elderly lady behind the counter was not fazed by the kyo-gai-jin (giant foreigner) who invaded her store, but set about giving me specific directions in rapid Japanese. To my delight I understood almost everything she said. I'm to go two blocks that way, turn left, go to the park, turn right, and can't miss it.

"Hai. Wakarimasu. Domo arigato gozaimas."

We exchanged smiles and slight bows and I was on my way, pleased with myself.

In the evening we are given another big party at the hotel. Whiskey, beer and wine are donated by the local liquor merchant. Lots of good food is spread all over the room. To my horror, a band of drummers is introduced and they go into their act with the usual deafening results. Perhaps they serve the same purpose at parties here as rock bands do at home. Once they start in, conversation is impossible and no one feels any pressure to be witty or make informed remarks. One can just relax and become a spectator. The party ends early because tomorrow we head for Russia.

**RACE STANDINGS AT SENDAI.** At this point 12,197 nautical miles from Montreal, the standings are:

### Turboprop

*Tiger*, the Cessna Conquest is in front, averaging 325.11 knots against a Vref speed of 311 knots. *Oak Lawn Express*, the other Conquest, is second at 320.97 knots and is 29 minutes behind. *Hors Ligne* is third and *Spirit of San Diego* is a miserable fourth, over seventeen hours behind the leader.

*Jan Roang, Bob Reiss and Poju Stephansen near Matsushima.*

### Turbocharged piston

The leader is *Go Johny Go*, the Cessna 210 that is averaging 198.97 knots against a Vref speed of 185. *Norway* is in second at 197.15 knots, followed by *Empty Pockets Express* (222.17 knots vs. Vref of 221 knots), *Kona Wind* is fourth, and *Spirit of 76* is last.

### Piston, normally aspirated

| PLANE | VREF | AVERAGE SPEED |
|---|---|---|
| 1. *Tail Wind World Flyer* | 170 knots | 176.43 |
| 2. *Zephyrus* | 216 | 216.84 |
| 3. *Cumulus Bound* | 198 | 194.53 |
| 4. *Spirit of Pacific* | 172 | 154.92 |

## FLASHBACK X

## "ONE OF OUR AIRCRAFT IS MSSING"

**MARCH 1956. TRAVIS AFB.** The call at the BOQ came at 0830 Sunday morning. Our hero had been in San Francisco the night before and hadn't returned until 0345. He was still hung over. "What?" he said into the phone.

"This is operations. Get into your flying gear and report here pronto. You and Captain Culver have to go over to Sacramento Airport and bring back a Globemaster that went in there last night on account of fog at Travis."

"Come on. This is supposed to be my day off."

"Tough. You're the only copilot available."

Grumbling under his breath and with no breakfast, the Lieutenant presented himself at Operations twenty minutes later. He and Captain Culver, along with two Flight Engineer Sergeants, hitched a ride over to Sacramento Airport on a C-47 just going out on a local training flight. Twenty minutes later they were dropped off at the Sacramento transient area.

Standing on the ramp the four of

them slowly turned 360 degrees as they searched the field.

"Could it be inside somewhere?"

"They don't have a hangar big enough."

"Then where could they hide it?"

"We'd better ask around."

They found a man on duty at the Flight Service Station. "What's a C-124 Globemaster?" he asked.

"Well, it's a real big Air Force airplane," said the Lieutenant spreading his arms out wide. "With a 172-foot wingspan, four engines and a tall tail, big doors in front, and about 200,000 pounds gross. Its serial number is 21080."

"Nope, can't help you. Nothing like that since I came on duty. You guys sure you've got the right airport?"

"Can we use your phone?"

Travis Operations was embarrassed. "There's been a screw-up here. The midwatch gang sent a crew over to Sacramento at 0500 and the plane is back here at Travis now. The dummies forgot to tell us about it when we relieved them this morning."

"Great! Well, okay, tell the C-47 to come back and pick us up."

"No can do. They just landed here with a rough engine and we've got nothing else in the area."

"How about a car and driver? We'll wait."

"None available. I guess you'll just have to get back on your own."

Two hours later the four airmen were on a crowded Trailways bus pulling out of downtown Sacramento for San Francisco and points in between. They were in flying suits and each carried his own headset and oxygen mask. Their fellow passengers kept staring at them. An elderly lady tapped the Lieutenant on his knee.

"Excuse me, young man, but have you boys been in a crash or something?"

"No, Ma'am," he sighed, "but it's a long story."

"That's all right, son," she smiled, "We've plenty of time."

# CHAPTER 11

# SENDAI

# TO

# PETROPAVLOVSK

THURSDAY, 19 MAY. We almost didn't get away. When we arrived at the Sendai Airport a Japanese Immigration official asked for our passports and we handed them over, as did several other crews. He then got in a car and went over to the main terminal on the other side of the field, where the passports would be given their exit stamps. Shortly after, two other Immigration officials showed up on our area and began on-site processing of the rest of the group. When they got to us we explained that our passports had been taken away and hadn't yet been returned. Confusion followed this, with officials phoning each other and warnings to us not to depart without our passports. (Don't worry, we have no intention of trying to enter Russia without them.) Our Bonanza is scheduled for an 8:30 a.m. departure and at 8:15 we are getting worried. The other lost passports have been brought over and returned to their owners, but not ours. More phone calls are made.

While we are anxiously waiting, I hear Bernard shouting at the top of his voice while he waves an invoice in his hand.

"For six box lunches and the cleaning of my chemical toilet they have charged me over $2,000. I refuse to pay!"

I am fascinated to see how this will turn out but before the coming confrontation a Japanese official tells us to get out to our airplane and prepare to leave. Our passports have been located and will be delivered at our airplane.

Passports aboard, we take off at 8:46 a.m. (2346 Zulu), cleared to Yalizova Airport, Petropavlovsk, at eleven thousand feet. The controller sets us climbing on a southeast vector of 120 degrees over the ocean. This is known as an "Aobar Reversal One" departure from Sendai and is specified for northbound flights at or above 9,000 feet for both noise suppression over the city and to coordinate traffic through the military airspace that lies to the north. We are vectored southeast for thirty-four nautical miles before being allowed to turn northwest and proceed back to the Sendai beacon. The beacon is recrossed at 0021 Zulu at 11,000 feet, and we are allowed to turn on course. It doesn't seem right to make an airplane setting off on a long difficult flight burn up thirty-five minutes of fuel before proceeding on course, especially when the weather prediction for our destination is poor and our alternate airport is Sapporo in northern Japan, very far from our destination.

While it's a crystal clear day here at Sendai, there is a low pressure system moving across the Sea of Okhotsk bringing low ceilings and rain. Terminal forecasts are all but impossible to pry out of the Russians so we have none for Petropavlovsk. They do, however, have an Instrument Landing System (ILS) there and that should help.

The weather gets worse steadily as we go north. We cross the waters between Honshu and Hokkaido, Japan's northernmost island, and pass over Chitose VOR (CHE) at 0206 Zulu, two hours and twenty minutes from departure. Our next checkpoint will be Monbetsu beacon (MV), our last Japanese navigation aid. Fifty miles beyond that we will be in Russian airspace and over the Sea of Okhotsk, beginning a seven hundred mile over-water flight to the tip of the Kamchatka Peninsula on airway G583.

Outside the cabin the air is getting rough. Clouds below us hide the ground from our view. The wind is from the northwest at 23 knots, not slowing us down much, but not helping either. Ahead we can see solid dark clouds that rise beyond our 11,000 feet. Turbulence is knocking us around. It is not steady but comes in violent spasms that bangs my head against the door frame overhead. I'm very glad that David Clark designed his headsets with a thick foam rubber cushion on top.

We have a new call sign for flying in Russia: "Race 5." Bob gets on the radio and tries to establish contact with the Russian controllers on 129.4 but gets no answer. Well, we hope they know we're coming. I have no idea what kind of a radio or telephone link the Japanese have with the Russian control center on Sakhalin Island, but those Russians are the boys that directed the intercept and shootdown of Korean Airlines flight 007 in 1983, so let's hope they aren't as gung-ho as they once were.

The dark clouds swallow us up and we settle in for what looks like a long session on the gauges. The outside air is holding at about plus five Centigrade so we are not threatened by ice yet, but we still have

three hours to go.

Off to our right about a hundred miles and unseen, lie the Kuril Islands, the chain of rocky and barren islands that runs from the tip of the Kamchatka Peninsula to Hokkaido. They were owned by Japan before the war and are a fertile fishing ground. The Russians declared war on Japan just two weeks before the Japanese surrendered to the Allies in 1945, seized the islands, and have held them ever since. Every year the Japanese make a formal request to discuss their return and every year the Russians refuse to answer them.

Russia is one of the few places in the world where flying is done in the metric system. Speed is in kilometers per hour, altitude is in meters, and airport surface wind is reported in meters per second. All of this is confusing unless you have handy conversion charts in front of you, which we do. I have also found that the D-4 computer I liberated from Anchorage Center in 1965, and carry in my jacket pocket to calculate time/distance problems can do feet to meters too. It's basically a circular slide rule and if you put the "10" on the inner wheel opposite the altitude in feet on the outer scale, then look where the inner wheel is marked "32," you can read almost the exact height in meters. The D-4 has printed on it "Property of the U.S. Army Air Forces" so I guess it goes back a few years.

Flying for long periods on instruments in solid clouds is always a kind of eerie experience to me. The autopilot handles the mechanical flying of the aircraft perfectly so there is no physical strain. Our only tasks are to adjust the course "bug" now and then to keep on the centerline, monitor the health of the engine, be alert for ice, and keep track of fuel consumption. There is no sense of movement in the clouds. The air is smooth and we just sit there listening to the engine and only imagining what the sea below looks like. For me, time passes like it must for a prisoner in solitary. There's not much to do except look forward to the next event that gives some structure to the day. For the prisoner it can be the next meal, a turn in the exercise yard, or a visit from the Chaplain. For me it is the next reporting point or course change. Time drags by.

Bob has out the approach plates for Petropavlovsk, which he studies intently. Like all Russian joint-use airports it has only one enormous runway, about 3,500 meters long and 150 meters wide. The ILS approach is from the southeast, from seaward and into the prevailing winds.

BUMEN intersection is a compulsory reporting point located astride the 150th East Meridian of longitude. It is not formed by navigation aids but is simply there on the charts, 404 miles southwest of Petropavlovsk. The GPS receiver in my hand had us over it at 0443 Zulu, an hour and twenty minutes ago. Bob gives the Russians a try again, this time taking the VHF frequency off the chart even though it warns us "Russian only."

"Petropavlovsk Control this is Race Five, over."

"Race Five, go ahead."

"Race Five over BUMEN at 0443, three thousand three hundred meters. Estimate SENOR intersection at 0619."

"Race Five, roger. Maintain three thousand three hundred meters."

Russian radios are different from ours. They still use vacuum tube technology. When their controllers open their microphones you can hear others talking in the control room, doors slamming, chairs scraping, etc. The controllers' accents are very heavy, but understandable. We should be thankful we can understand them at all. Most of them have little opportunity to practice their English in this part of the world.

As we get closer to landfall we begin to hear other racers on the frequency. We cross SENOR at 0618 and are over land at Ust-Bolsheretsk beacon (UB) at 0624. Now we turn to heading 081 degrees for the 152 kilometer (82 NM) crossing of the Kamchatka Peninsula. All of Kamchatka is volcanic mountains. I have out my ONC chart and study once again the local terrain that is still invisible to us. Just ten miles north of Yalizova Airport is a 12,000 foot monster volcano, Mt. Koryakskaya. The field elevation of the airport is only 131 feet so there must be a dramatic view of it on a clear day.

At least two of the Arc en Ciel aircraft are claiming low fuel and are requesting priority handling for approach. I recognize the voice of Jim Knuppe in his Cessna Citation. The Yalizova weather sounds bad. The latest report we heard was ceiling overcast at 200 meters (640 ft.), visibility 800 meters (one-half mile) in rain, wind 260 degrees at four meters per second (about 8 mph). The Russians are getting confused down there. The pleas for priority handling are met with long silences. They begin taking the

Americans one by one, giving them radar vectors toward the ILS approach.

Soon we are radar identified and told to descend to 2,200 meters (7,000 ft.). Bob is off the autopilot now and is hand-flying the Bonanza on instruments. We are turned to a course that will intercept the ILS localizer at 90 degrees and require us to make a left turn for the airport at that time.

Suddenly, without warning, a very excited Russian voice is in our headsets.

"Race Five, emergency descent to one thousand meters. Start descent now!"

"Race Five, roger." Bob reduces power drastically and drops the landing gear. "Race Five leaving 2,200 meters." We start sinking at 1,000 feet a minute.

"Race Five, what is your altitude?" This only thirty seconds later.

"Race Five passing through 2,100 meters."

"Increase rate of descent now, Race Five!"

Now we are going down at 2,000 feet per minute.

We will find out later that the aircraft on approach ahead of us (Cumulus Bound) had flown through the ILS centerline inadvertently and was preceding, still on instruments, in the general direction of Mt. Koryakskaya. Upon realizing what had happened they abruptly turned 180 degrees and were flying back toward the localizer and head-on with us. (American airmen, once given a radar heading to fly, will fly it until told to turn, or at least given a warning that a turn is coming up. This doesn't seem to be the practice in Russia.) Now the controller had himself a classic glitch and he was resolving it in the first way that occurred to him.

"Race Five, report altitude!"

"Race Five passing 1,700 meters."

Race Five, roger, descend to five hundred meters."

Every time the controller asks our altitude — about every thirty seconds — I read the altimeter in feet, spin my D-4 computer and shove it in front of Bob's nose with my thumbnail pointing out the altitude in meters for him to read back. All this is not good for the nerves.

"Damn it!" says Bob as he realizes we, too, have flown through the localizer, although just barely. He bends the airplane in a 45-degree bank to the left and takes a heading to reintercept the centerline. Both of us had been concentrating on the descent and not noticed the quick movement of the localizer needle.

"Race Five, report altitude."

"Race Five, leaving 850 meters." (2,700 ft.)

"Race Five, descend to 200 meters now."

Whoa! That's only 600 feet and we're still sixteen miles from the airport. I have the GPS receiver set for Yalizova (UHPP) and by pressing the "GO TO" button I can get a bearing, distance and course line indicator from our present position direct to the center of the airfield at any time. I push the button now and give Bob the new bearing. We're way below the steep ILS beams now and Bob gives up on them.

At just above 700 feet we break through the base of the clouds. We're over farming country and flying in light rain. The GPS shows we are heading for the airport, eight miles ahead. I quickly unfold my ONC chart and scan for obstacles. I know the Russians are big on TV towers and smokestacks but I don't see any southeast of the field on the map. That doesn't mean much however, this map says on its corner that the data used to compile it was gathered in 1956. This is no way to run a Russian Far East railroad! You could definitely bust your ass here — but good. We are both straining our eyes through the windshield trying to penetrate the rain and clouds as we seek the field hedgehopping along on this contact approach. The controller has given up on us. He is no longer asking for altitude or anything else. He's probably just sitting at his console figuring we are lost in the ground clutter of his radar and keeping his fingers crossed that both planes will have enough separation to avoid arriving at the end of the runway at once.

The farms have thinned out and suddenly the runway end is in sight. Bob drops the flaps and makes his usual skillful landing on the large wet surface and we slow down and turn off where directed. Whew! I'm glad that's over. I offer up a "Well done, sir" to Bob. He has remained amazingly cool throughout the hairiest approach I've ever experienced, and kept the Bonanza under perfect control at all times. It was a fine demonstration of the art of instrument flying.

The landing was at 8:06 p.m. (0706 Zulu). It is still broad daylight here at almost 53 degrees north latitude. Our flight time from Sendai has been seven hours and twenty minutes.

We taxi along for what seems like two miles to the civilian terminal area, passing numerous revetments in which are parked large Russian Navy amphibious flying boats, turboprop powered and twin-tailed. We park, get out and go through Customs. They have thoughtfully dragged over an airport tram, used to haul passengers to and from the airliners, and set up shop inside so we can be processed out of the rain. The officials seeing to us are military, not civilian, and I am reminded that this city, Petropavlovsk, is an important submarine base and military airfield. Foreigners like us were not allowed to come here at all until just a few years ago. The Russians don't look particularly happy to see us now.

There are two buses waiting for us but not all our aircraft have arrived yet. Bob uses the time to fuel the Bonanza in the cold drizzle and wind. The remaining racers arrive one by one. Many of them have their own exciting story concerning their approach and landing at this strange place.

Our bus finally departs the airport but we don't head for the city. Our haven for the next two nights is to be the Spa Kamchatka, a health resort about twenty-five miles out in the country. It is still the tag end of winter here with three to four feet of melting snow on the ground. Pine and birch trees cover the landscape. It looks very much like parts of Alaska.

We reach the Spa Kamchatka. It's a two-story L-shaped structure bearing a close resemblance to a World War II military barracks. Inside, the decor can best be characterized as Depression-era Flophouse. We are shown to our quarters. Each room sleeps two and each two rooms share a bath. The bath has two sub-units — one compartment is a toilet and the other holds a sink and the strangest shower I have ever seen. It is a raised concrete circle, about two feet off the floor, with a drain in the center. Above it is a small spigot about three feet higher. One must have to squat, frog-like, on the concrete to use the spigot and take great care not to splash about for there is no shower curtain. Bob and I stare at it suspiciously for a few minutes.

The dining room is open and we are hungry. The waitresses look stern as they serve their guests. There is no menu or choice of entrées and we are served some kind of extra crispy fried cutlet along with a cucumber salad. Bob and I had quite a bit of experience with Siberian cuisine in 1992 on our trip through Russia and it was our general experience that no matter how bad any one meal was, there was always at least one dish served that was pretty good. Tonight this good thing comes in the form of a platter of smoked salmon. It's oily and delicious and we both rip into it.

The day has been one of considerable strain for all the fliers and many grab this chance to relax around the tables and swap stories of their day's experiences. Others, younger and adventurous, go outside to try the thermal waters of the spa in a large steaming pool. This hotel is a place where people come to seek relief from their arthritis or other ailments in the therapeutic hot waters. How arthritic patients get up and down from the second floor without an elevator or use the showers in their room I can only imagine. In any case, there aren't any of them here now. We seem to have the hotel to ourselves. Knowing Bernard and the high quality of our hotels on this trip so far, I have to assume that this place is the best Petropavlovsk has to offer.

After the meal is over, the cook, wearing his tall chef's hat, and all hot and sweaty, comes out of the kitchen and sits on a stool in the corner beaming at the strange foreigners that have invaded his world.

Kamchatka doesn't see many tourists and we will find ourselves to be objects of curiosity for the next day or so.

When we retire to our room we find the beds so short that we both have to sleep in the fetal position. The toilet seat's hinge is broken and when I lift it up the seat falls on my bare foot causing great pain. Someone has been making plumbing repairs next to the toilet and there's a large deep hole in the floor next to the john. When you turn on the light, cockroaches scurry back into the hole. Welcome to the Spa Kamchatka!

FRIDAY, 20 MAY. Neither of us is brave enough to risk his neck in the shower, so sponge baths are in order. Breakfast in the dining room is a plate of yogurt and some kind of mush. I immediately dub it "curds and whey" and the name catches on.

We board a dubious looking bus for a tour of the city. It's a cold gray day with a low ceiling and occasional rain. Everyone is wearing his/her heaviest clothing. On the outskirts of Petropavlovsk we stop for a few minutes beside the monument to Vitus Bering, the Dane in the service of Peter the Great who was the first European to explore this part of the world. He founded this city in 1728 and named it the same as his two ships, the *St. Peter* and the *St. Paul*. His explorations led to the Russian occupation of Alaska.

Our bus drops us off at the city historical museum, a poorly lit and cluttered collection of artifacts. The native inhabitants of the Kamchatka Peninsula are close cousins to the Alaskan Eskimos, and the museum has many examples of their crafts and artwork on display.

The next stop is City Hall for lunch. The city of Petropavlovsk-Kamchatsky (there's another Peter and Paul in Kazakstan) has a population of about 100,000 and has all the sparkle and charm one expects of a Siberian arc-

*May 20th at Spa Kamchatka, Petropavlovsk, not the racers' favorite accommodations.*

*This is the monument at Petropavlovsk commemorating the achievements of Vitus Bering.*

omy one must remember that the ruble is worth 100 kopeks, and the kopek is in the process of being devalued to a more realistic zero.

Lunch over, Bernard holds a press conference in one of the City Hall meeting rooms. There's about six members of the local media in attendance. Bernard goes through his usual remarks about how there are no borders visible from the air and how general aviation brings all people together as brothers. When he opens the session for questions a Russian newspaper woman, speaking very fluent English, surprises everyone in the room by asking Bernard about his Arc en Ciel sponsored Trans-Atlantic race in the 1980s where one of the race planes was lost and the crew killed. Would he care to comment?

The young newswoman has evidently been doing her homework. Bernard is taken aback but recovers quickly. He explains that the aircraft in question probably suffered a complete electrical failure over the Atlantic and, alas, its fate is unknown. The clear implication of the question was that international air racing is a dangerous and foolhardy sport for rich capitalists with nothing better to do. [She may have an arguable point here, although the same conclusion could be reached concerning mountain climbing, auto racing, parachute jumping, big

tic outpost. Drab Russian apartment complexes surround the center of the city. A giant statue of Lenin still overlooks the town square. Melting snow has turned into a brown slush that covers everything. The deep harbor is full of rusting freighters and factory fishing boats. The new free economy of Russia has led to a number of entrepreneurs who are selling food and merchandise from the backs of vans parked on the streets. It seems a cheerless place. These hardy people have been through a political and social upheaval, and they still have a long way to go. To understand their econ-

*A city scene in Petropavlovsk.*

*A statue of Lenin in the background at Petropavlovsk.*

game hunting, or any other human endeavor involving challenges and risks.] Bernard wisely avoids this type of debate and moves smoothly to the next questioner.

Sightseeing and press conference over, we head back to Yalizova Airport for a weather briefing for tomorrow's flight to Anchorage, Alaska. Out in the countryside our bus breaks down. The driver, obviously an old hand at this, soon has his body's upper half buried in the engine compart-

*Some of the fishing vessels, freighters and buildings at Petropavlovsk Harbor.*

ment while the rest of us stand on the roadside trying to keep warm. We get going again after half an hour.

The bus finally arrives at Yalizova Operations and we begin getting off. The weather has cleared enough that we become aware of a looming presence not seen before. It is Mt. Koryakskaya, all 12,000 feet of it, snow covered, and dominating the northern horizon only ten miles away. This almost perfect cone is not like Everest or McKinley, a higher peak among other peaks, but a mountain standing alone on a flat plain. It seems to rise to infinity. It is both beautiful and awe-inspiring. As each person gets off the bus he or she sees the others frozen in place, staring upwards, and turns to do likewise. Soon, our entire group is standing dumbfounded by the gigantic volcano.

"Jesus! To think that thing was out there when we arrived yesterday," says someone. "I'm almost glad we couldn't see it. It would have scared me to death."

Our weather briefing, conducted by the head meteorologist, a female PhD named Olga, goes swimmingly. She has a set of large weather maps, scientifically drawn, that prove we will be blessed with fair weather and tailwinds all the way to Anchorage. Bob and I are suspicious. On our previous flight through Siberia it was our experience that if you were fortunate enough to get any kind of a weather briefing at all, the Russians were prone to tell you what they thought you wanted to hear, regardless of the actual situation. I don't know why they do this. Perhaps it is a way to get rid of these foreigners without having to answer a lot of annoying questions.

The bulk of the meeting, however, is devoted to the special departure procedure designed just for us. The easiest way for eastbound flights to leave would be to simply fly over the city and harbor where there are no obstacles and head out to sea on their way to Alaska. But that would take them over the submarine base and other secret installations where the CIA agents, doubtlessly among the crews, could photograph everything. None of this is stated, of course. All is smiles and goodwill. Instead we are to take off and fly northwest into the mountains until well clear of all ground installations before turning eastward on airway G583 and proceeding on course. To accomplish this a complicated procedure has

*Bob Reiss standing at the Yalizova Airport in Petropavlovsk.*

*The beautiful Mount Koryakskaya near the Yalizova Airport. It was a stunning sight.*

been devised to allow our heavily loaded aircraft to climb into the mountains with some safety. We are to take off on runway 34, climb for two minutes, execute a standard rate right turn of 185 degrees and head directly for the radio beacon PR located three miles south of the runway. Once there, we will turn right to heading 340 degrees again and track on another beacon, PK, located one mile to the north-west of the northern end of the runway. If we can cross PK at 1,900 meters (6,000 ft.) or above we are okay and can continue. If not, we are to fly in a right hand racetrack pattern between PK and PR until we can. Once past PK we are to head north for a point located at coordinates N53.31.4 E158.12.2, cross it at or above 3,000 meters (9,700 ft.), and then turn right to 061 degrees and begin tracking on airway G583. This arbitrary point must have a name for reporting purposes. By unanimous consent we name it "Olga" in honor of our meteorologist. The Russians hand out crude but clear handmade charts of the departure route for our use.

Back at the Spa Kamchatka a party has been pre-pared. There are at least a dozen Russian guests, over half of them in military uniform. The Spa has opened a shop in a shed near the dining room and is dispensing vodka ($20 a bottle, U.S. dollars cash, thank you), and some really vile limeade mix to go with it. There are many speeches and toasts into the night. Even the waitresses are smiling for a change.

## FLASHBACK XI

## "ALL WET"

In the 1950s all C-124 Globemaster crewmen in Pacific Division MATS had to attend a three-day Survival Training course once a year. They were scheduled in groups of twenty. It was held at Hickam AFB, Territory of Hawaii. They were taught about Jungle Survival ("Watch the monkeys and eat what they eat."), Arctic Survival ("Try to conserve body heat if you can.") and Desert Survival ("It helps if you have lots of water with you."). But the really fun part of the course was Ocean Survival, a subject of some interest to the men since they all spent a lot of time over the Pacific.

First, they got to open up a huge twenty-man life raft and play with all the toys inside. There was a hand-cranked "Gibson Girl" generator to power an HF radio and a kite to run up the long antenna, a complete fishing kit, a first-aid kit, a solar powered still for making fresh water, waterproof boxes of rations, canned water, a floatable knife, signaling mirrors, and tubes of sunburn cream.

When that was done they all went over to the Officers' Club swimming pool to practice setting up a raft in the water. Those who had attended the course before always selected a newcomer to be the one to jump in first, receive the raft in the water, and pull the inflating lanyard. When the victim was in the pool, treading water, six others grabbed the raft and started swinging it back and forth.

The collapsed raft was six feet long, two and a half feet in diameter, and weighed close to three hundred pounds. With all the equipment inside, it could barely float.

"Are you ready?" (swinging the raft)

"Sure! Let's have it." (arms outstretched)

"One, two, three, Go!" They would toss the raft as high as possible. When it hit the swimmer the man and raft would plunge nine feet directly to the bottom of the pool while air bubbles rose from each of them. Then, very slowly, both would rise to the surface with the victim half drowned. This was the signal for the rest of the class, fully clothed, to leap into the pool (Yippee!), inflate the raft, and spend the rest of the day setting up the still, flying the kite, making eyes at any nurses sipping drinks around the pool, and generally having a good time.

Fortunately, neither our hero nor anyone he knew, ever had to actually ditch a C-124 into the ocean.

# Chapter 12

# PETROPAVLOVSK TO ANCHORAGE

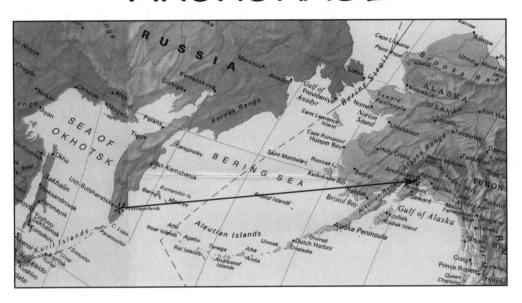

SATURDAY, 21 MAY. Although we have arrived at the airport by 8:00 a.m. there are many bureaucratic delays before we are allowed to depart. The authorities have asked each crew to stand in front of their plane with all their luggage for inspection by Customs. The wait seems endless.

Nancy Law of *Empty Pockets Express* goes around among the planes asking for the loan of articles of clothing. Their Navajo Panther's heater doesn't work and they can't get it fixed until Anchorage. She and Dave Sherrill are freezing in the cockpit. We manage to come up with a spare set of heavy gloves for them.

The local weather is clear as predicted, so at least we won't have to fly the "Olga" departure procedure on instruments. One by one, the racers are allowed to depart. Only after each crosses PK at or above 1,900 meters is the following aircraft cleared for takeoff. It turns out that Dr. Willie Tashima and Herb Halperin are the only ones that have to do an extra lap to make the crossing altitude.

It's eleven in the morning before we start the engine. Another day half shot by delays. We make a long taxi to the departure end of runway 34. Bob keeps it slow because we started with 65 gallons in each tip-tank and the taxiway is full of large potholes. He carefully maneuvers around them. My general impression of Russia is that no one ever maintains anything. We are cleared onto the active runway and cleared for departure. But wait! We're not on the runway yet. We're on the overrun at least 200 feet from the beginning of the runway and it's all full of holes like the taxiway. Bob "rogers" the clearance but continues rolling slowly around the holes until we are on the concrete runway proper before bringing in the power.

Our takeoff is at 11:24 a.m. (2224 Zulu) and the cold air gives us plenty of lift. Two minutes after takeoff we reverse course and head south for PR which I have tuned in on the ADF and also set as a waypoint on the GPS. At PR we turn north again towards PK and cross it at 7,500 feet with room to

*The view from N9675R over the Kamchatka Peninsula after departure from Petropavlovsk.*

spare. We're on our way! Next stop is the United States, over 1,700 nautical miles away. When planning this leg months ago, I drew up several alternative plans for us to land and refuel in Anadyr in Siberia, or in Nome, Alaska. But those are dismissed now. We both have every confidence in the Bonanza and its ability to take us nonstop anywhere within a 2,000 mile range.

With all the complications of the departure behind us I have a chance to look around at the scenery. The giant cone of Mt. Koryakskaya is behind us now, off to our right. Ahead lie endless ranges of tall mountains. The entire landscape is covered with snow, even down in the deep valleys. On the far horizon I can see several active volcanoes with smoke drifting from their craters. This is truly a pristine wilderness, silent and all but inaccessible to man.

Thirty-four minutes after departure we are at intersection OLGA, level at 4,100 meters (13,000 ft.) as we turn on course for Alaska. My chart shows the minimum terrain clearance for this portion of G583 is 14,600 feet but there's no point in worrying about it on such a clear day as this. Many of the peaks pass close beneath us as we fly along. If an aircraft went down out here in these mountains I have no idea what the Russians could do about it.

We are flying along in smooth air when we both get a shock. A shadow briefly darkens the Bonanza as a higher and faster racer passes over us. We look up and see a Cessna 210 Centurion about a thousand feet above us. It's Poju and Jan, the two Norwegians, passing us. Bob gives them a hail on the radio and chats for a few minutes. This activity attracts other listeners and soon a lively chatter is going back and forth. *Tail Wind World Flyer*, with the mother and daughter crew of Marion Jayne and Pat Keefer, is on frequency, too, and Pat reminds everyone that today is her mother's birthday. Bob knows Marion is from Texas and decides to give her a birthday present by singing a chorus of "The Yellow Rose of Texas" to her over the radio but he can't recall the words. I have a trick memory for lyrics so I write the words down for Bob and he warbles away for a couple of choruses much to Marion's amusement.

A little over an hour has passed since our departure and we begin to see an end to these tall white mountains. At 2336 Zulu we pass the coastline and begin our long crossing of the Bering Sea. Our next landfall will be the west coast of Alaska, 1,080 nautical miles away. The weather is thickening too. A deck of stratus clouds obscures our view below. Through occasional holes I can see that almost solid floe ice covers the surface of the water. There is no doubt that we are close to the Arctic Circle. The outside air temperature is dropping, too.

At 0032 Zulu we reach DALUV intersection which is at the boundary between Petropavlovsk-Kamchatsky and Tilichiki Flight Information Regions. We try again to make a position report but can't raise anyone. Well, that's nothing new on this trip. Our next compulsory reporting point is BESAT intersection which is 475 nautical miles to the northeast and is the dividing line between Russian and United States airspace. Our ground speed is down to 170 knots with the wind almost dead on our nose at 10-11 knots. So much for the predicted tailwinds all the way.

It's the middle of the afternoon. The cloud deck below us has been slowly rising and is now only about 3,000 feet below us. The sky above is relatively clear with some wisps of mares' tails high overhead. My eye is caught by a strange phenomenon below and to the right of the plane. It's a large reddish-orange ball of light, traveling along with us on the surface of the clouds below and exactly matching our speed. It's not bright enough to hurt one's eyes but is more like the glow you see in the middle of a burning fireplace. In the center of the ball I can see the perfect shadow outline of the Bonanza, small and well defined. It's a sundog! I've heard of them before but never experienced one myself. Fascinated, I watch it on and off for an hour before it disappears.

BESAT intersection is reached at 0317 Zulu. That's just after 6:00 p.m. local time. When we pass BESAT two things happen at once: (1) we pass into U.S. airspace, and (2) the International Date Line is crossed and today becomes yesterday.

Bob gets busy on the radio. "Anchorage Center, this is Bonanza 9675 Romeo, BESAT."

"Bonanza 9675 Romeo, Anchorage Center, go ahead."

"75 Romeo, BESAT at 0317 Zulu, Flight Level 130, estimating Bethel at 0627."

"9675 Romeo, Anchorage Center. Roger your position and estimate. Are you one of the racers?"

"That's affirmative. Our authentication number is Foxtrot 674."

"Don't know about that. Are you landing Merrill Field?" [This means the ICAO flight plans carefully filed at Yalizova operations have not been passed on by the Russians. Just as in 1992 when we passed this way before, the entire North American Air Defense System has been surprised by a string of small aircraft.]

"Affirmative. Request clearance from present position direct Bethel, Victor 319 Sparrevohn, Victor 508 Merrill."

"Roger your request. Squawk 1734 now.

"Roger 1734 now."

"ATC clears Bonanza 9675 Romeo to Merrill Field via direct Bethel Victor 319 Sparrevohn Victor 508. Maintain flight level 130."

All the argle bargle aside, it's very good to hear an American air traffic controller's voice again.

Two hours later the sun begins to set in the long northern twilight. Without the solar heating from the sun the cabin temperature is getting cold. Shudders hit me every so often as the chill gets to me.

"How about some cabin heat, Bob?"

"It's full on now."

Oh, oh. All I'm wearing is a wool shirt and a medium weight flying jacket while Bob has prudently brought an arctic parka which he is now wearing. I've brought a set of thermal underwear two-thirds of the way around the earth for a moment just like this but didn't put it on this morning because it seemed such a nice sunny day. Now the underwear is in my bag, stowed in the rear of the airplane and out of reach behind the auxiliary tank. I'll just have to tough it out. What I don't realize is that I am experiencing the early stages of hypothermia. My feet, hands, and head are all right (I'm wearing thick socks, gloves, and a wool watch cap), but the cold is invading my torso. The shudders continue.

The darkness comes on slowly as we approach the Alaskan coast. We ask for and receive a terminal forecast for the Anchorage area. It is expected to be IFR with an 800-foot ceiling and one and one-half miles visibility. That means we will probably not go into Merrill Field, the general aviation airport, but will shoot an ILS into Anchorage International, land, and then fly over to Merrill when the weather improves.

We make landfall fifty miles south of Cape Romanzof. Bethel lies 100 miles ahead. Although we can't see it because of the clouds, the land below is flat treeless tundra, filled with lakes and slow rivers. The mountains lie ahead, nearer Anchorage.

I'm getting sleepy. My mind seems to drift off every now and then. It seems we have been in the air forever and this flight is going to have no end. I long either to go to sleep right here or else stand up and bend my legs and swing my arms around. Just sitting here is...

"Dennis. Are you all right?" asks Bob.

"Yeah, yeah. Just a little cold that's all."

I shake my head, take a drink of water, and try to concentrate on the task at hand. My left knee is aching pretty bad but I don't try to straighten it out. The pain helps me stay more alert.

We cross Bethel VOR (BET). Anchorage is 340 nautical miles ahead, two hours away. The clouds are changing. In the lingering twilight (it never gets fully dark in late May at 61 degrees north latitude) we can see huge cumulus buildups ahead as the air currents rise from the Kuskokwim Mountains. The outside air temperature is minus 24 degrees Centigrade and there's a good chance of ice inside the clouds so Bob intends to stay clear of them as much as he can.

We make Sparrevohn VOR (SQA) at 0732 Zulu and shortly the minimum en route altitude on V319 jumps to 12,000 feet as we approach the Chigmit Mountains, the last barrier between us and Anchorage. The cloud buildups reach higher, too. We can see the tops ahead are at least a thousand feet higher than we are and there's no way around them. Bob turns to me.

"I'm going to request 15,000 feet for awhile so we can get over these tops. I'm going to go on oxygen but your mask is somewhere back there and I can't find it. Think you'd be all right for half an hour or so?"

"Sure!" I'm a bit euphoric anyway.

Bob requests and receives clearance to 15,000 feet and we sail over the tops in our path.

At TORTE intersection, 50 miles from Anchorage, the airway minimum altitude drops back to 6,000 feet meaning we are past the tallest mountain peaks. Merrill Field is now reporting visual conditions as we are turned over to Anchorage Approach Control. A smooth and pleasant female voice speaks to us.

"Bonanza 9675 Romeo, Anchorage Approach. Radar contact. I will vector you for a visual approach to Merrill Field, runway 08, Anchorage altimeter, 29.63. Descend and maintain 7,000."

As we let down we enter a cloud layer. Both of us begin checking our side of the aircraft for signs of ice. There is a slight buildup of rime on the leading edge of the wing and the nose of the tip-tanks but it doesn't seem to get any worse as we move down into warmer air. I do notice, however, that with each pulse of the wingtip strobe light I can see a circular pattern of ice crystals in the air for the microsecond the light flashes. I mention this to Bob.

"Oh. Does that bother you?" he asks. "Here, I'll fix it." And he reaches over and turns off the strobes!

I'm feeling a lot better now that we're down where it's warmer. The controller clears us down to 3,000 feet and we break through the ceiling and see the lights of Anchorage up ahead. She has us lined up perfectly with the east-west runway at Merrill. It's only 4,000 feet long so we don't dare be high or hot on the approach. Bob drops the gear, puts down half flaps, and slows to approach speed. He brings it over the threshold just right, lands on the first third of the runway, and goes into BETA (reverse thrust) with the prop. We slow to taxi speed with room to spare. Petropavlovsk to Anchorage has taken ten hours and eleven minutes. The local time is thirty-five minutes after midnight on the morning of Saturday, 21 May, the same day we left Russia.

We get through U.S. Customs and Immigration, eat some cold pizza left over from some other crew's arrival party, and head wearily for the Sheraton Hotel and rest.

SATURDAY, 21 MAY (AGAIN). We both sleep in until 7:30 a.m. I call my oldest daughter, Irene, and invite her to breakfast. She is a corporate attorney presently detailed to Anchorage for six months serving on the defense team at the civil trial concerning the wreck of the tanker *Exxon Valdez* and the subsequent oil spill in Prince William Sound. (Hey, even big bad oil companies are entitled to a defense, and Exxon can afford the very best.)

*Willie Tashima and Herb Halperin after spending the night in King Salmon, Alaska.*

At breakfast we get some alarming news. Dr. Willie and Herb made an emergency landing last night in King Salmon, on Alaska's west coast, after they ran into severe icing and are now stuck there until the weather improves. I feel I had a part in this. Back in Petropavlovsk, while we were doing some flight planning, Willie had expressed his concern for ice on this trip, especially over the mountains. I pointed out to him that he had an alternative. He could go a little further south, over King Salmon, and avoid the higher mountains. There, where the minimums are much lower, one could stay low and perhaps avoid getting into freezing levels. Now, it looks like Willie might have taken my advice and got himself in a heap of trouble. At least they're both safe.

Later in the day Bob and I hang around downtown Anchorage for awhile. It sure looks different from when I lived here during 1962-65. Then it had a population of fewer than 40,000, including the military presence. Now the population exceeds 125,000. They even have freeways. I suggest to Bob that we visit the offices of Reeve Aleutian Airways and look at their collection of photographs on the history of Alaskan aviation. We seek them out and find several office rooms with their walls covered with pictures of early bush pilots, daring rescues, and the early airlines of America's Last Frontier. The office manager graciously takes an hour of her time to conduct us on a tour of the collection. It's the same all over. If one aviation history buff recognizes a similar spark in another, they suddenly have time to spare to show you what they have and share it with you.

In the evening Irene joins Bob and me for the combination press conference and group dinner at the Sheraton. Just as the affair is getting under way, in come Willie and Herb, still in their orange flying suits, just in from King Salmon. They certainly seem to be the group's designated hard luck team. We're all glad to see them.

Bob has already notified Bernard Lamy that we will not be continuing on with the group to Calgary and Montreal, but have decided to head home from here to San Diego. We have never really been in the race and there is little point in flying all the way to Montreal just to turn around and fly back to San Diego. Ironically, this evening is the only one since the race began where we win any kind of a prize. Because we have flown nonstop between Petropavlovsk and Anchorage and not refueled at Nome as one of the other turboprops did, we have somehow come in third out of four planes for that leg. Our prize is an eskimo ulu, a special knife used for flensing dead seals.

We say our good-byes to all the racers and wish each of them good luck.

## RACE STANDINGS AS OF ANCHORAGE

| PISTON POWER (NORMALLY ASPIRATED) | % OF REF SPEED | TIME BEHIND |
|---|---|---|
| 1st *Tail Wind World Flyer* Twin Commanche | 101% | |
| 2nd *Zephyrus* Glasair III | 99% | 1:32:36 |
| 3rd *Cumulus Bound* B58 Baron | 97% | 3:48:06 |
| *Spirit of Pacific* Bonanza | (not placed) | |

PISTON (TURBOCHARGED)

| | | | |
|---|---|---|---|
| 1st | *Go Johny Go* | 106% | |
| | Cessna 210 | | |
| 2nd | *Norway* | 104% | 1:25:00 |
| | Cessna 210 | | |
| 3rd | *Empty Pockets Express* | 99% | 4:30:36 |
| | Navajo Panther | | |
| 4th | *Kona Wind* | 84% | 16:09:18 |
| | Cessna 421 | | |
| 5th | *Spirit of 76* | 77% | 25:54:56 |
| | Cessna 340 | | |

TURBOPROPS

| | | | |
|---|---|---|---|
| 1st | *Tiger* | 103% | |
| | Cessna Conquest | | |
| 2nd | *Oak Lawn Express* | 102% | 0:28:00 |
| | Cessna Conquest | | |
| 3rd | *Hors Ligne* | 92% | 9:50:04 |
| | Cheyenne I | | |

# FLASHBACK XII

# "BUT THAT CAN'T HAPPEN! CAN IT?"

JUNE 1956. The C-124 Globemaster took the active runway at Wake Island under rainy skies. The copilot read off the last of the pre-takeoff items from the scrolling checklist in front of him.

"........Doors and hatches closed, shoulder harnesses locked. Pitot heat coming on. Checklist complete."

"Right," said the Aircraft Commander. "Let's do it. Max power."

"Max power," echoed the flight engineer.

The aircraft began its ponderous takeoff roll. Four thousand feet down the runway the airspeed indicator showed 106 knots and the pilot gave the elevator trim a one-eighth turn and eased back on the wheel to lift the nose into rotation position. A moment later the plane left the ground.

All of a sudden the engineer began shouting. "Numbers 2 and 3 losing power! Number 1 — No! — number 4 — I mean total loss of power on all four!"

The Globemaster settled back down on its still extended landing gear. About a thousand feet of runway remained. The pilot stood on the brakes, but it wasn't easy to stop a hundred tons of airplane doing ninety miles an hour. As the last of the runway disappeared beneath the wheels, he shouted, "Prepare for crash!"

The plane hit the crushed coral runway overrun, used that up, crossed a road, slowed down some as it ran over a hard sandy beach, and finally came to a shuddering stop in the surf of the Pacific Ocean with a great spray of water. Waves broke over the wing roots as the crew collected themselves. "Everybody all right?" asked the pilot. Everybody was.

The tower had seen nothing because of the rain. Wake Departure Control was making futile attempts to contact them on the radio. Everyone was confused.

"What the hell happened?" asked the pilot. "How could all four engines quit at the same time?"

"I don't know," answered the engineer. "It's not supposed to happen that way."

The answer to the question came much later. The aircraft had taken on a load of ADI (Anti-detonation Injection) fluid after landing at Wake. This is the stuff sprayed into each cylinder during takeoff (and only during takeoff) to prevent overheating. Almost never called for at Wake, the storage tank had rusted over the years and severely contaminated the fluid.

The crew was rescued after the copilot swam to shore and hailed a passing truck on the perimeter road. The aircraft, thoroughly soaked in salt water, was a total loss.

# CHAPTER 13

# ANCHORAGE TO SITKA

SUNDAY, 22 MAY. At eight o'clock in the morning Bob is on the phone in our hotel room to the local Flight Service Station. A giant low pressure storm has moved into the Gulf of Alaska with its center about 250 miles south of Anchorage. Winds are at gale force and severe icing is forecast from 1,500 to 12,000 feet. Filing a regular IFR flight plan to Ketchikan is out of the question. All the airways leading southeast from Anchorage have to clear the mountains and their minimum en route altitude is 10,000 feet. On our 1992 world trip we had ourselves a true emergency when we attempted to climb IFR on airways leaving Anchorage and ran into severe icing at 9,000 feet. We managed to get out of it in one piece but it gave us both a good scare.

The sensible decision would be to wait until the weather improves but the forecaster says this storm isn't going anywhere for at least three days. The local weather is VFR under a solid overcast at 3,500 feet. Getting out of Anchorage will be no problem. The trouble lies farther south.

"Well," says Bob, "if we can't go through it, maybe we can go under it. We could stay over water all the way and it may be possible to do the whole thing VFR."

I pull out the WAC charts for this part of the world. Yes, it does look plausible. If we head southwest from Anchorage and fly down the Cook Inlet we can round the Kenai Peninsula and enter the Gulf of Alaska through the Kennedy Strait. Once in the Gulf we can head almost due east and, staying over water all the way, cross to the beginning of the Alaskan Panhandle at Ocean Cape. South of there we can stay offshore and, one hopes, fly into better weather.

Using an old-fashioned flight plotter (basically a protractor with a straightedge attached) I draw the course lines on the map and carefully write down the latitude and longitude of each course change point right next to its location on the chart. Now we have all the waypoints for the GPS.

We check out of the hotel and get over to Merrill

Field. Merrill has little call for jet fuel and they don't have a truck. We taxi over to their jet fuel pump and a few minutes after fueling begins, the tank goes dry on us. The racers started very early this morning and got all the fuel first. Now what? Bob calls Signature at Anchorage International, and they agree to send a jet fuel truck clear across town, at least ten miles, just for us. Nice folks. The truck arrives after half an hour, fills us up, and the driver departs with a fat tip in his pocket.

What with one thing or another, we have used up the entire morning, but that's not important. We shouldn't be in the air for more than seven or eight hours and sunset comes very late up here at this time of year. We taxi out to the runway. It's only 4,000 feet long and there's no overrun at the end — an industrial park begins where the runway stops. We get no route clearance this time. We're going VFR.

"75 Romeo, cleared for takeoff."

"75 Romeo."

Bob positions the Bonanza at the very end of the runway and takes the engine to full power while standing on the brakes. We begin the takeoff at 12:09 p.m. local (2009 Zulu). It's cool in Anchorage (about 44° F) and the propeller takes a good bite in the air. We lift off with at least 500 feet of runway to spare and make a shallow climbing turn to the southwest to pick up airway V334 that goes to the town of Kenai. We level off at 1,200 feet. Five minutes after takeoff we are clear of Anchorage and over the gray waters of the Cook Inlet. The land on either side of the inlet is flat and the air is smooth under the solid ceiling of clouds. It's always a treat to fly cross-country this low. Every detail on the ground is clear and there's a real sense of speed as you pass over the surface of the earth.

We pass Kenai and the Cook Inlet widens out as we leave the shore behind. Eighty nautical miles later we are abeam the southernmost tip of the Kenai Peninsula and I give Bob a new heading of 099 degrees which should take us through the passage between the tip of the Peninsula and the Amatuli Islands. As we negotiate the passage into the Gulf of Alaska I can see ahead that the ceiling is lowering and the clouds are much darker. We're approaching the edge of that monster storm.

Thirty minutes later we are really into it. Turbulence, heavy rain and a 40-knot wind from the northeast are beating on us. Bob has gone down to

900 feet in an effort to keep visual contact with the surface which by now is a maelstrom of huge waves with flying spume streaming off their crests. At 900 feet these waves appear threateningly close to the aircraft as they break and curl just below us.

This is getting downright exciting!

The rain, which seems to come in squalls, hits the Bonanza so hard and heavy on occasions that the airframe actually flinches from the force. The air inlet to the engine has its own heater, and it's turned on, but how much water can a jet engine swallow without putting the fire out? The air temperature is holding at plus six degrees, so ice is not a problem. Personally, I made sure to don my thermal underwear this morning and I am toasty warm in the cockpit.

The high winds have pushed our ground speed down to 135 knots. It's going to be a long crossing of the Gulf. Between the rain squalls, visibility is about a mile and a half. At 900 feet we are hard up against the black clouds that form the solid ceiling. Occasionally we pass through the bottom of a distension from the mass above us. In or out of clouds we are legal. We are below Alaskan controlled airspace and no authorization is needed to fly here from anyone.

One of our waypoints is Middleton Island, sitting out alone in the Gulf. They have a VOR/DME (MDO) on the island along with an airstrip. That means there are probably people there.

"You know Bob, I was just thinking. We have no idea what kind of radio antennas or other rigs they have on Middleton. We're at 900 feet now but we might be forced lower. Why don't we pass the island five miles to the south and that way be sure we clear everything?"

Bob agrees with this reasoning so I alter course accordingly. When we go by Middleton all we see are some outer rocks, awash in the storm.

Three hours into the flight and there's no end to this tempest. We are bouncing around from the turbulence so hard that Bob, normally on his fourth cup by now, has not dared to open his thermos of hot coffee in the cockpit. The winds have come around to dead on our nose and have reached true gale force.

We are now bucking a headwind of 75 knots! Our ground speed is registering as low as 94 knots. Twice now we have flown over fishing boats. The waves are enormous and when the boats crest into one of them half their hull is exposed to the air before they pitch over for a wild vertical ride down the slope, then repeat it all over again. How the crews take it I'll never know.

My thoughts dwell for a moment on the consequences of an engine failure out here. At this altitude we would be lucky to get off an emergency "Mayday" and position report before we hit the water. If we survived the ditching (a big "if") and the aircraft held together, the tip-tanks might keep us afloat long enough to deploy the raft and get into our immersion suits. If not, then our life expectancy tables would drop dramatically. Better not to muse on this. Get back to navigation.

We are close enough to shore now that Bob can raise the Flight Service Station at Yakutat and get local weather along the panhandle coast to the south. It seems that amidst this giant weather system only two stations are reporting marginal VFR conditions: Yakutat itself and Sitka. The others, Juneau, Wrangell, and Ketchikan included, are operating under instrument conditions. We more or less give up on Ketchikan at this point as a destination for today. It is located to the east of Alaska's Inside Passage and is situated in a bowl surrounded by mountains where the initial approach is 6,000 feet. We need something where we can sneak in below the icing level. We'll keep checking the weather as we go along.

The point I have arbitrarily picked for our turn to the southeast is at N59.20 W140.10, about twenty miles southwest of Ocean Cape. As we near it the

*A part of downtown Sitka in Alaska.*

*Another view of Sitka.*

rain squalls let up and visibility improves greatly. Ahead, we begin to make out the shoreline marked by steep snowcapped mountains reaching up into the still solid overcast. The town and airport of Yakutat are located there, right on the shore, but we still have four hours of fuel remaining, even with the head winds. The Sitka weather is holding just above VFR minimums and is forecast to remain so. The airport is located on Baranof Island, about 200 miles from here, with direct access from the waters of the Gulf of Alaska. It's beginning to look like Sitka is it for today.

After our turn southeast the weather holds for a while, then gets nasty again. We are about thirty miles from shore, still at 900 feet, and paralleling airway V440 on a track of 113 degrees when the rains hit again. The noise on the aircraft's hull is very loud and at times all visibility, forward or down, is lost in the almost solid downpour.

My terrain chart for the Alaskan coast shows that Sitka Airport is placed north of the city on the shore of a bay with an entrance about four miles wide. Mountains surround the bay on three sides. The entrance to the bay is guarded to the north by Cape Edgecomb which extends five miles out into the Gulf. Near the tip of the Cape sets Mount Edgecomb, 3,600 feet high, an obstacle to be avoided at all costs.

I select a point on the map, N56.45 W135.50, that will put us clear of Cape Edgecomb and give us a straight shot at the airport through the entrance to the bay. I don't know what the visibility offshore will be and I want a way we can enter the bay blind if need be. I double check the coordinates on the chart for the second time before punching them into the GPS receiver. Then I check them again.

Bob, watching all this, says "That's the third time you've done that."

"Yeah. It's as if our lives depended on it."

Bob gets the point.

We hit the checkpoint and I enter the identifier for Sitka Airport (PSIT) in the GPS and hit the "GO TO" button. Sitka is reporting 1,100 feet ceiling, visibility three miles in light rain. As we pass through the bay entrance the visibility improves markedly and we can see the buildings of the city on our right and the airport straight ahead. Snowy mountains form a ring around the whole setting. The landing is routine at 6:45 p.m. (0245 Zulu). The flight from Anchorage has been 767 nautical miles in six hours, twenty-nine minutes. The fierce headwinds have given us an average ground speed of 110.6 knots.

We secure the Bonanza for the night and, upon the recommendation of the local fixed base operator, take a cab to the Shee Atika Hotel. I treat Bob this night to the best steak dinner in town. He's earned it today. That was as nifty a piece of airmanship as I have seen in a long time. He is now referring to it as his "Charles Lindbergh" flight.

## FLASHBACK XIII

### "A FLIGHT TO NOWHERE"

OCTOBER 1956. The Lieutenant (our hero) had now logged over 1,000 hours of C-124 time. He had passed his check ride as a first pilot, and was certified eligible to fly as Aircraft Commander on domestic flights out of Travis AFB. He had also been promoted to the lofty rank of lst Lieutenant. All this was heady stuff and he now awaited his first assignment as pilot-in-command. It came within two weeks.

"You're on for a 2030 departure tomorrow," said the Squadron Dispatch officer. "Your co-pilot will be Lt. Kramer, and your engineers will be Sgts. Weston and Hawthorne."

"Great! What's the cargo and where are we going?"

"I can't tell you because I don't know — it's classified. You'll be briefed at 1930 tomorrow. No need to pack an overnight bag."

The next evening the briefing officer gave him the mission. "We've filed an IFR flight plan for you from here to El Paso. The weather will be clear. Ten minutes before El Paso you are to cancel IFR with Air Traffic Control and then call over El Paso at 7,500 feet on frequency 266.3 identifying yourself as 'Big Boy.' You will be answered by 'Boss Man' and radar identified. After that, just do whatever 'Boss Man' tells you to do. Don't talk to anyone about this, including your crew, until you are airborne. There'll be two additional passengers in the cargo area."

As the crew boarded the aircraft via the nose door, the two "passengers" turned out to be a pair of Army troopers, in full battle gear, standing in front of a curtain that shielded most of the cargo deck from view. They ascended the ladder to the flight deck in silence.

Four hours later, in a clear but moonless sky, they were over El Paso. "Boss Man, Boss Man, this is Big Boy. How do you read?"

"Big Boy, this is Boss Man, loud and clear. Turn left 90 degrees for radar identification."

They were given a long series of random headings to fly. After a while there were no more lights to be seen on the ground. After forty-five minutes of this the Lieutenant and the rest of the crew had no idea where they were. Were they still in Texas, or in New Mexico? They might be south of the border for all they knew. Eventually, they were instructed to descend and run through their check lists, then to deploy their landing gear and flaps. At the last moment a set of runway lights was illuminated in front of them. As soon as they landed the lights went out. A "Follow Me" truck came out of nowhere and they trailed it to the ramp and shut down on command.

As his feet hit the ramp, our hero became aware that the aircraft was completely ringed by Army personnel in red berets armed with automatic weapons. A spotlight hit him in the eyes, ID's were checked. An Army Captain said "All of you follow me." The Lieutenant did not argue.

The four were marched over to a building and placed in a locked room with two guards. They were not offered coffee. After ninety minutes they were marched back to the aircraft and told to depart. The cargo deck was now empty.

The same aimless vectoring was given them as they climbed out. After a long interval "Boss Man" said, "You should be able to see the lights of El Paso by now and receive their VOR signal. You're on your own. Thank you, and out." They returned to Travis about dawn.

Its been forty years since that night and the Lieutenant still doesn't know where he went or what he carried on his first trip as pilot-in-command.

# CHAPTER 14

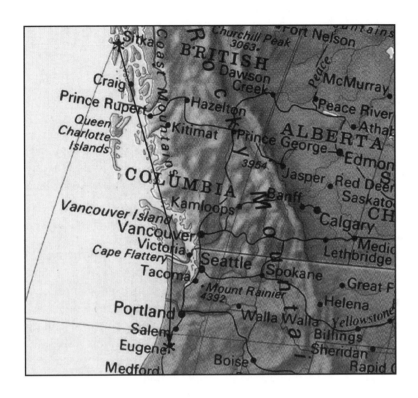

# SITKA

# TO

# EUGENE

MONDAY, 23 MAY. From Sitka to San Diego it is almost exactly 1,700 nautical miles. We could do that in one hop if we chose to but we both realize how tired we are. There's no point in pushing ourselves any longer. We are free of the race group and its rigid schedule and can set our own pace now. We decide that Eugene, Oregon, a little over half way home, would be a reasonable destination for today. After a leisurely breakfast we check the weather by phone from the hotel. It's still bad. The storm is stationary with strong winds and freezing levels down to 5,000 feet. We even contemplate another low-level offshore flight and I go so far as to plot coordinates on the chart when Bob thinks better of the whole thing. This is an international flight through Canadian airspace and we should try to do it by the book. He files an IFR flight plan to Eugene via V440 Victoria V495 Portland V23 Eugene.

We lift off the Sitka runway at 11:18 a.m. (1918 Zulu) and start climbing into the overcast. Our track is 122 degrees from the Biorka Island VOR (BKA)

on airway Victor 440 whose minimum en route altitude is 12,000 feet, which is our assigned level. If we run into ice in these clouds our escape plan is to turn right, leave the airway, and descend out to sea picking up our offshore way-points as we go.

Climbing through 9,000 feet we both see rime ice forming on the wings and tanks. It's coming on fast and something must be done — right now.

"Anchorage Center, this is Bonanza 9675 Romeo at 9,000 feet, experiencing moderate to heavy icing."

"75 Romeo, roger. Descend and maintain minimum terrain clearance altitude of five thousand six hundred feet to Port Hardy. Advise when clear of ice."

Twelve thousand is the minimum altitude to ensure good reception of the VOR airway beams along this rugged coast where the stations are over 200 miles apart. Fifty-six hundred is the minimum terrain clearance altitude where, if you stay within the confines of the airway, you are guaranteed to

113

clear all mountains. As we descend, the accumulated ice on the wings begins to crack and peel off.

It's a shame to fly the length and breadth of this most beautiful of states and not see anything more than an airport or two, but that's the hand we have been dealt on this trip. We continue, on instruments and guided by the GPS, toward the Canadian beacon at Sandspit, almost 200 miles away. The wind is still on our nose at 35 knots as we continue to fly the outer rim of this immense counter-clockwise storm system.

Three hours of instrument flying later, we are approaching Port Hardy on Vancouver Island, British Columbia. Both the American and Canadian controllers we have been talking to over this period have shown great concern regarding our icing situation and have checked with us every fifteen minutes or so for a "howgozit" report. Our worry right now is that after Port Hardy the minimum terrain clearance altitude on V440 goes up to 9,100 feet for the 108 miles of airway to Comox. We have been checking the weather ahead and realize that we are approaching the southern limit of this storm that we have been screwing around with for two days.

"Bonanza 9675 Romeo, Vancouver Center. Climb and maintain 9,100 feet. Report any icing."

"9675 Romeo, roger. Leaving 5,600."

The outside air temperature is now a more reasonable 8 degrees Centigrade, so maybe we can reach 9,100 feet before it drops below freezing. This proves to be the case and within ten minutes we are at cruise altitude and all is fine.

At Comox the clouds begin to break and we catch occasional glimpses of green mountains below. Twenty miles north of Victoria we finally fly into the clear. It's always a splendid view here when the weather is nice. Victoria is below with its fine harbor and the Empress Hotel, and over to the east is the city of Vancouver. Ferries ply Puget Sound and one can just make out Seattle to the south. Once past Victoria we are handed off to Seattle Center.

"Seattle Center, this is Bonanza 9675 Romeo, request clearance present position direct Eugene at 9,000 feet."

"75 Romeo, roger your request. Stand by."

Bob waits patiently but the requested clearance is not forthcoming. There's no use in flying directly through the congested Seattle area unless you intend to land there.

"Seattle Center, 9675 Romeo, Cancel IFR."

"75 Romeo, roger, cancel IFR."

We drop down to 7,500 feet as I program the GPS for Eugene Airport and press the "GO TO" button. The Olympic Peninsula is its usual magnificent self off to our right with its snowcapped mountains,

The Puget Sound area gives way to the rolling rich farmlands and forests of Washington and northern Oregon. Eugene lies halfway between the Washington and California borders in the valley of the Willamette River. It is prime farming country. The airport is the perfect model of a modern airport with its new tower, broad ramps, and twenty-four hour services for general aviation aircraft. We land at 6:47 p.m., six hours and twenty-nine minutes from Sitka. An hour and a half later we are in the Valley River Inn, dog tired. We book separate rooms to get away from each other's snoring for one night. A nearby Domino's delivers a large pizza with extra pepperoni, then we call it a day.

*Part of the airport and runway at Eugene, Oregon.*

# CHAPTER 15

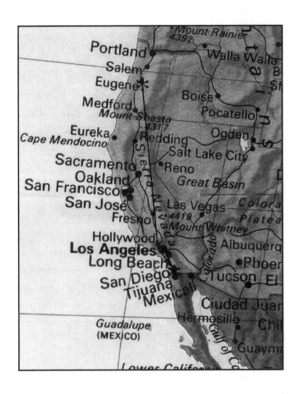

# EUGENE

# TO

# SAN DIEGO

TUESDAY, 24 MAY. It's a clear warm day in Eugene, perfect for flying. A check with the FAA weatherman shows we can expect clear skies all the way to San Diego, a (now) trifling 761 miles to the south. We depart VFR at 10:15 a.m. A hundred miles south of Eugene the mountains begin. We cross into California and the perfect cone of Mt. Shasta looks down on us from its 14,000-foot peak in the Cascade Range. An hour later we are in the Sacramento Valley with the still snowy Sierra Nevada off to our left. Redding, Chico, Marysville, then into the San Juaquin Valley. Merced, Chowchilla, and almost directly over the huge twin runways of the Naval Air Station, Lemoore.

Bob chooses to enter the Los Angeles area via the Cajon Pass thereby staying away from the Terminal Control Area. As we near the pass the smog rising out of the San Bernardino and Riverside areas looks as solid as granite. We sink into it with all four eyeballs pressed against the windows looking for other traffic, and get the latest Montgomery Field, San Diego, weather. They are reporting below VFR conditions with a ceiling of 800 feet broken, and 1,200 feet overcast. Visibility is six miles in light haze.

*The majestic Mount Shasta in Northern California.*

*Journey's end for the Author and Bob Reiss — happy but tired and glad to be home. Bob rightfully gestures toward the star of our trip, his A36 prop-jet Bonanza.*

Well, how about that? Not only was the forecast wrong this morning but so far we have gotten completely around the world having shot only one real instrument approach (Petropavlovsk). It's ironic that the second one will be at San Diego, home of good weather.

Fifty miles north of San Diego Bob contacts Southern California Approach and requests an ILS into Montgomery Field. We are over a solid deck of clouds at 7,000 feet as the controller vectors us to the approach for runway 28. Bob informs me he is going to shoot this one on automatic with the ILS receiver coupled to the autopilot. He's never done this in actual weather before, always preferring to hand fly the plane. The autopilot handles it perfectly, with the localizer and glideslope needles forming a perfect crosshairs and not moving a bit until we break out on final and Bob releases the autopilot.

Touchdown is at 3:12 p.m. (2212 Zulu), four hours, fifty-seven minutes from Eugene.

The circumnavigation has taken us twenty-nine elapsed days from San Diego, but because of the International Date Line, we have seen thirty sunsets. Flying time has been one hundred twenty-six hours, twenty-seven minutes and

we have covered 21,352 nautical miles. It's been no vacation, but it sure has been a wonderful adventure!

Bob has called ahead with our approximate arrival time and as we taxi up to the hangar a small party of friends and mechanics form a greeting committee. After handshakes and congratulations all around, Bob and I stand a moment and contemplate Bonanza 75R. She is filthy from her trip but given a fresh load of jet fuel, could start out again right now. Her few squawks (wing light and fuel pump warning light) have been minor and she has consumed only two quarts of engine oil on the entire trip. She is a standing tribute to the design and engineering genius of American aircraft makers.

We are glad to be home. After all the work of preparation, and as long as the Global Positioning System kept working, the navigation portion of the flight was relatively easy. The real credit for the success of the venture rightly belongs to Bob Reiss. He has been the spiritual (not to mention financial) sparkplug that made the flight possible, and his skill and resourcefulness as a pilot have brought both of us back home again, not only safely, but, I like to think, as better people and better friends.

---

### RACE WINNERS

The winners of the FAI medals were:

PISTON (NORMALLY ASPIRATED)

| | | |
|---|---|---|
| Twin Commanche N33226 | Marion Jayne | USA |
| *Tail Wind World Flyer* | Patricia Keefer | USA |

PISTON (TURBOCHARGED)

| | | |
|---|---|---|
| Cessna 210 N5531W | Erik Banck | Belgium |
| *Go Johny Go* | Merce Inglada | Spain |

TURBOPROP

| | | |
|---|---|---|
| Cessna Conquest N1210U | Vijaypat Singhania | India |
| *Tiger* | Daniel Brown | USA |
| | Peter Troy-Davies | UK |

# EPILOGUE

After a flight like this one, it seems a bit odd just to go back to your ordinary routine. Friends and relatives have heard about it, of course, and most want to hear more, but if they are not aviation people themselves they don't know how to ask questions and you soon find yourself in a one-sided monologue that you eventually cut short out of fear of boring the other person.

The only publicity we got was a two-page story with photos in the *Pacific Flyer*, a monthly aviation newspaper. An unexpected and welcome result of this story was a contact from my old roommate in Primary Flight Training at Hondo, Texas, Jack Farrar, who now lives in Texas. We had been out of touch for forty years.

Bob, with his reputation as a public speaker, has been asked by a number of organizations to come and give a talk about world flying. He has put together a slide show combining the 1992 world flight and this one and has made scores of presentations to civic and aviation groups. Now and then I go along and give a short talk on the navigational aspects of long-range flying. These sessions are a lot of fun. Bob has also become a contributing editor to the journal of the World Beechcraft Society on the technical complexities of long-range flying. He is rightfully considered an expert in this area.

One of the most important spinoffs of all this for me personally was a renewed interest in the history of aerial navigation, especially the early Atlantic flyers. This led eventually to my applying for training as a docent at the San Diego Aerospace Museum where I now am a volunteer tour guide two days a week and derive much satisfaction from teaching others about a subject I love.

What else did I learn from all this? Well, I found some places on earth I had never been to before, and having experienced them, never intend to go near them again (Agra, Ho Chi Minh City, Petropavlovsk). Other locations have found a place in my heart and if time and funds permit, I will gladly go back and spend awhile getting to know them better (St. John's, Azores, Malta, Istanbul, Okinawa). The bad side of a journey such as this is that you are focused out of necessity on the flying, and not on the people and places you are flying over.

The other thing I have learned is that even older folks can enjoy a challenge now and then. There's a lot more to life than being safe and comfortable. A part of the human spirit contains an eagle — and that eagle wants to soar.